GREEN FINANCE IN CHINA

中国绿色金融

2018年第1辑 [总第1辑]

主办单位：中央财经大学绿色金融国际研究院
支持单位：中国金融学会绿色金融专业委员会

中国金融出版社

责任编辑：肖　炜
责任校对：张志文
责任印制：程　颖

图书在版编目（CIP）数据

中国绿色金融（Zhongguo Lüse Jinrong）.2018年.第1辑：总第1辑：汉英对照/王遥主编. —北京：中国金融出版社，2018.5

ISBN 978 – 7 – 5049 – 9544 – 5

Ⅰ.①中…　Ⅱ.①王…　Ⅲ.①金融业—研究—中国—汉、英　Ⅳ.①F832

中国版本图书馆CIP数据核字（2018）第068707号

出版　**中国金融出版社**
发行

社址　北京市丰台区益泽路2号
市场开发部　　（010）63266347，63805472，63439533（传真）
网上书店　http://www.chinafph.com
　　　　　　　（010）63286832，63365686（传真）
读者服务部　　（010）66070833，62568380
邮编　100071
经销　新华书店
印刷　北京市松源印刷有限公司
尺寸　205毫米×267毫米
印张　6.25
字数　144千
版次　2018年5月第1版
印次　2018年5月第1次印刷
定价　35.00元
ISBN 978 – 7 – 5049 – 9544 – 5
如出现印装错误本社负责调换　联系电话（010）63263947

中国绿色金融
Green Finance in China

中国绿色金融（第一辑）
Green Finance in China （First Collection）

主　　编：王　遥

责任主编：刘苏阳　卢　刚

编　　译：陈　京　刘阳洋

审　　定：Mathias Lund Larsen　Phillip Roin

Chief Editor：Wang Yao

Executive Editor：Liu Suyang　Lu Gang

Translator：Chen Jing　Liu Yangyang

English Proofreader：Mathias Lund Larsen　Phillip Roin

目　录

1　　　推动中国资产管理绿色化　　　　　　　　　　　　马　骏　王骏娴
11　　　Promoting the Greening of Asset Management in China　　Ma Jun　Wang Junxian

25　　　中国绿色金融发展趋势展望及银行业在其中的作用　　　　周月秋
30　　　Outlook on Development Trends of China's Green Finance and Roles of
　　　　Banking Sector　　　　　　　　　　　　　　　　　　Zhou Yueqiu

37　　　中国绿色资产证券化的现状分析及发展建议　　　　　　　周亚成
45　　　Analysis of Current Situation and Development Suggestions on
　　　　China's Green Asset Securitization　　　　　　　　　Zhou Yacheng

58　　　加快绿色证券化进程　　　　　　　　　　　　Michael Sheren
62　　　Accelerating Green Securitisation　　　　　　　　Michael Sheren

66　　　绿色金融的国际趋势与中国的领导地位　　　　　Scott Vaughan
72　　　International Trends of Green Finance and China's Leadership　Scott Vaughan

80　　　中国绿色金融体系的发展回顾与展望　　　　　　　王　遥　罗谭晓思
85　　　The Progress and Outlook of China's Green Financial System
　　　　　　　　　　　　　　　　　　　　　　　　Wang Yao　Luo Tanxiaosi

推动中国资产管理绿色化

■ 马　骏　王骏娴[1]

摘要：资产管理的传统理念是在投资者给定的财务风险偏好或约束下取得最好的财务回报，环境因素不是资产管理者考虑的内容。但是，近年来资产管理的绿色化正在成为一个新的趋势。所谓资产管理的绿色化，是指资产管理者在投资决策过程中充分考虑投资所带来的环境、社会影响和环境因素对投资回报的影响，以减少对污染和高碳资产的投资，增加对清洁、低碳资产的投资。

由中国倡议发起并共同主持的G20绿色金融研究小组在2016年的《G20绿色金融综合报告》（以下简称《综合报告》）中明确指出了绿色金融发展的几大趋势，其中包括机构投资者的绿色化。近年来，中国国内的绿色金融业取得了快速进展，人民银行、证监会等七部委联合发布的《关于构建绿色金融体系的指导意见》明确提出了要引导机构投资者开展绿色投资，鼓励机构投资者开展环境风险分析。这些意见正逐步演化成具体的措施、方法和工具，未来会对市场产生深远的影响。

本文对资管行业绿色化的背景、绿色投资策略、环境风险管理、环境压力测试等问题进行深入探讨，提出相关政策建议。

一、资产管理绿色化的背景

当前气候、环境因素对经济社会可持续发展的制约越来越大，全球面临着由高污染、高耗能、高排放的经济发展模式向绿色低碳经济转型的迫切要求。为了应对这些挑战，各国政府相继出台相关政策，积极推动经济转型。我们的研究显示，污染型和高碳的经济发展模式源于污染型和高碳的产业结构，而污染与高碳的产业结构则主要源于污染型的投资。导致大量污染型投资的深层次原因包括绿色投资的激励机制缺失和一系列制约绿色投资的体制机制弊端。

---

[1] 马骏为清华大学金融与发展研究中心主任、中国金融学会绿色金融专业委员会主任，中国人民银行研究局前首席经济学家。王骏娴为中证金融研究院研究人员。

为解决这些问题，我国正在推出央行再贷款、贴息、担保、政府基金等支持绿色投资的激励机制。但是，在财政能力有限、而绿色投资需求巨大的情况下，仅仅靠政府的激励机制是不足以推动投资绿色化的。资产管理行业管理着巨大的私人部门资金：截至2016年底，全球机构投资者管理着约100万亿美元的资产；在中国，机构投资者管理着116万亿元人民币的资产[1]。这些资产的管理者如果没有绿色偏好，过度投资于污染性和高碳资产，则经济绿色化转型就是一句空话。换句话说，资产管理的绿色化在构建绿色金融体系的过程中将起到关键的作用。

资产管理的绿色化是指机构投资者在投资决策中充分考虑环境因素，以减少对污染和高碳资产的投资，增加对清洁、低碳资产的投资。在一些成熟资本市场中，早期资产管理机构的绿色投资起因于受托责任。受托责任要求资产管理人确保实现资产所有者的利益或诉求。由于部分资产的所有者（如宗教资金、养老金）等提出了投资中考虑气候、环境等因素的诉求，使得其资产管理者开始关注绿色投资。例如，荷兰医疗保健养老金（Pensioenfonds Zorg en Welijin, PFZW）宣布将在2020年前其可持续投资（绿色能源、清洁技术及水短缺防范技术等）达到160亿欧元，同时将投资组合中的碳足迹降低50%。最近几年，社会舆论的要求、NGO的推动，以及巴黎协定、G20倡议的政策信号等因素都在帮助强化绿色投资的理念。在我国，绿色投资的理念更多地源自政府的推动，包括"两山"理论、《生态文明体制改革总体方案》《关于构建绿色金融体系的指导意见》等决策和文件。

二、责任投资原则（PRI）

在上述力量的推动下，越来越多的机构投资者开始关注绿色和责任投资原则。2016年的《综合报告》提出，作为绿色金融发展的一项具体内容，各国可在自愿的基础上考虑推广和采纳联合国责任投资原则（UN Principles for Responsible Investment，PRI）等绿色金融准则，并强化PRI等机构的能力建设功能。

PRI要求机构投资者清晰认识到环境、社会和公司治理（ESG）问题，倡导在投资决策过程中应充分考虑环境、社会和公司治理因素。绿色金融中的"绿色"，即环境因素，是责任投资需考虑的三大因素之一。责任投资原则包括六条具体内容：

1. 在投资分析与决策过程中考虑环境、社会和企业治理（ESG）因素；

2. 在行使股东权力时强化对环境、社会和企业治理（ESG）因素的关注；

3. 要求被投资机构披露环境、社会、企业治理（ESG）方面的信息；

4. 促进投资业接受并实施责任投资原则；

5. 建立合作机制，提升PRI原则实施的效果；

6. 披露执行责任投资原则的实施行动和取得的进展。

责任投资原则发起于2006年，在此基础上成立了名为联合国责任投资原则机构。自提出以来，该原则受到了来自国际上许多机构投资者的积极支持。2006年，全球责任投资原则的签署机构仅为100家，管理的总资产为6.5万亿美元；而

---

[1] 数据来自前瞻产业研究院。

截至2017年6月，签署机构数为1715家，管理的总资产超过62万亿美元。签署机构最多的地区是欧洲和美国，分别为696家和256家，来自新兴市场国家和地区的签署机构数量上升得也很快，最新的数据包括巴西的57家、南非的52家和中国（包括中国香港）的23家[1]。这些签署PRI的机构投资者包括了全球许多主流资产管理机构，如黑石集团、加州公务员退休基金、德意志资产与财富管理、安联欧洲公司、英国耆卫保险、巴西银行养老基金、日本政府养老基金、韩国国民年金和加拿大退休金计划等，中国的华夏基金管理公司和易方达基金管理公司也在其中。

此外，由联合国环境规划署金融倡议（UNEP FI）联合发起，PRI作为支持单位的低碳投资组合联盟（Portfolio Decarbonization Coalition，PDC）聚集了追求低碳目标的27家大型机构投资者，包括瑞典第四国家养老基金（AP4）、东方汇理资产管理公司、法国巴黎资产管理公司等。PDC倡导投资者采取系统化的措施，使投资组合符合低碳要求，如减少投资组合的碳足迹、增加可再生能源领域的投资、从高耗能活动中撤资、鼓励所投资企业减少碳排放、支持低碳经济转型等。据PDC2016年的年报显示，全部27家成员机构已积极开展减少投资组合碳足迹的行动，其中17家机构已披露了部分或全部投资组合碳足迹的指标。

在我国，中国金融学会绿色金融专业委员会（绿金委）、证券基金业协会、中证金融研究院等机构于2016年7月与联合国责任投资原则机构合作开展了对国内机构投资者的首次关于责任投资的培训活动，得到了60多家机构投资者的欢迎，此后又就此议题举办了多次研讨活动。绿金委、商道纵横联合多家机构在过去几年联合举办的责任投资论坛也在不断推广责任投资原则、工

具和方法。

三、绿色资管的投资策略

PRI从资产所有人与资产管理机构的关系、资产管理机构与被投资者之间的关系等角度提出了一系列推动绿色和责任投资的基本原则。落实到具体的资产管理工作，尤其是一个资产管理机构的首席投资官、首席风险官和基金经理们，他们在投资策略和方式上到底要做哪些变化呢？从国际经验来看，机构投资者开展绿色投资的投资策略和方式主要有七种类型：

（一）黑名单机制

黑名单机制即将环境风险或ESG风险较大的资产从投资组合中剔除。例如在投资决策时设定一些标准，将污染性或高碳企业的股票或债券排除在可选投资标的之外。例如荷兰APG资产管理公司（APG Asset Management）将所有石化类股票剔除其投资组合之外。安联欧洲股份公司（Allianz SE）取消了对煤炭行业的投资。

（二）白名单机制

白名单机制即选取具有较好环境表现的行业和公司进行投资。例如荷兰医疗保健养老基金（PFZW）挑选绿色能源、清洁技术、食品安全和水资源行业中碳减排成效最佳的企业进行投资。再如兴业全球基金，建立了一个绿色股票库，并根据企业履行环境责任的情况进行综合打分和排名，从中筛选出优秀的企业进行投资。

（三）ESG策略

ESG策略即在原有的投资策略中加入环境或ESG因素。例如，资产管理公司可以在原有开展资产配置或选择资产的模型、方法的基础上，加

---

[1] 见www.unpri.org。

入ESG评级指标（不少评级指标可从Bloomberg或MSCI获得），使资产配置或选择股票、债券的结果变得更加绿色。

（四）绿色指数投资

绿色指数投资即被动投资于一些绿色指数产品，包括低碳指数、新能源指数、ESG指数、环保指数等。目前国际上绿色指数已有数百种，比较著名的如S&P 生态指数、MSCI 环境指数。国内也有21只绿色股票指数和16只绿色债券指数，部分指数已经被用来做成基金产品。例如海富通中证内地低碳经济主题指数证券投资基金跟踪标的为中证内地低碳经济主题指数，交银施罗德国证新能源指数分级证券投资基金跟踪国证新能源指数。

（五）绿色主题投资

绿色主题投资即投资某一类或几类于绿色和环境相关的主体或产业。比如，一些机构发起了绿色建筑基金、清洁能源基金、专注污水处理的环保基金等。丹麦养老基金ATP投资了可再生资源和清洁能源部门相关的企业股权和债权，并向气候变化基金注资 10 亿欧元，以投资于新兴市场国家；前海开源清洁能源主题混合型证券投资基金通过精选投资于清洁能源主题相关证券，在合理控制风险并保持基金资产良好流动性的前提下，力争实现基金资产的长期稳定增值。

（六）社会影响力投资

社会影响力投资（Social Impact Investment）是指在追求财务回报的同时，争取获得环境和社会效益的投资。这类基金投资的对象包括环保、应对气候变化、扶贫、教育等。这类投资基金有的也被称为社会企业，社会企业要求将其利润的大部分再投入到社会和环境公益事业中。目前参与此类投资的以家族慈善基金、养老金等为主，其他社会资本也在逐步加入。

（七）股东参与

股东参与即机构投资者代表资产所有人行使股东权利，影响被投资企业的环境和社会表现。比如，股东可在股东大会就企业的环境相关议题行使权利，督促企业更注重环境责任和信息披露；与企业高管层沟通，要求公司积极参与绿色投资，减少污染性活动等。如管理一百多亿美元的Hermes基金管理公司，通过积极影响被投资企业的ESG表现，取得了很好的长期财务回报。

根据全球可持续发展投资联盟（The Global Sustainable Investment Alliance，GSIA）的数据显示[1]，截至2016年全球有约22.9万亿美元的绿色与责任投资，相比2014年上升了25%。此类投资占全球投资规模的26%。目前国际市场上绿色与责任投资占比较大的三个地区是美国、加拿大和欧洲。增长速度最快的三个地区是日本、澳大利亚、新西兰。全球占比最大的投资战略是黑名单机制，其次是整合ESG策略。除了日本以外的亚洲其他国家的责任投资总体市场增长速度较慢，到2016年总规模约521亿美元。运用较为普遍的是整合ESG策略，其次是黑名单机制。

根据万得（Wind）系统的数据统计，目前我国资产管理中绿色与责任投资约123亿美元（注：由于各国统计口径不一，这个数字与GSIA的数据不可比）。虽然可比统计尚不可得，但从调研的情况来看，我国机构投资者开展绿色与责任投资的情况还不普遍，与国际前沿（尤其是欧洲）还有较大差距，同时也表明未来我国绿色与责任投资市场发展潜力很大。

---

[1] 见GSIA 2016年全球可持续投资报告。

表1 全球绿色与责任投资（2016年）

单位：十亿美元

地区	资产总额	占本地区投资总额的比例	占全球绿色与责任投资总额的比例
欧盟	12040	52.6%	52.6%
美国	8723	21.6%	38.1%
加拿大	1086	37.8%	4.7%
澳大利亚&新西兰	516	50.6%	2.3%
亚洲（除日本）	52	0.8%	0.2%
日本	474	3.4%	2.1%

数据来源：GSIA。

四、环境风险分析与管理

分析和管理环境风险是资产管理业开展绿色投资的一个主要内容。有效识别和管理环境风险，有助于资产管理公司规避由于环境因素所导致的股票估值下降和债券违约等下行风险，从而提供资产组合的长期回报率。这些风险分析的集合（宏观）意义是推进金融业减少对污染和高碳行业的资产配置，增加对绿色产业的配置。

（一）风险分类

2017年G20绿色金融小组提出了金融市场主要面临的两类环境风险分别是物理的环境风险与转型相关的环境风险。

1.物理风险

物理风险是指由于污染和气候变化等因素导致的对人类和经济活动的破坏性影响。这些风险来自空气污染、水污染、土壤污染、自然灾害、气候变化、水资源短缺、自然资本退化等。气候变化与各种自然灾害的关系密切，前者会大幅提高各类自然灾害发生的频率。

许多行业，如农业、矿业、旅游业、远洋捕捞业等，受气候风险（如水灾、干旱、飓风、台风）的影响较大。海平面上升、全球升温以及突发性的水污染、土壤污染等事件也会影响许多行业和企业。这些风险会导致企业产能下降、成本上升、劳动力缺失、固定资产提前报废、建筑物受损及需求下降等。

2.转型风险

转型风险是指由于包括政策和监管力度变化、碳价格上升（可能由政府减少配额所导致）、技术变化、声誉损失等主要由人为因素导致的风险。比如，由于环境监管力度加大和碳市场的引入，高排放企业面临环保罚款上升、购买碳配额的成本增大等风险，从而会导致利润减少、估值下降、违约率上升。也有一些政府会提高对污染物排放的税费，或开征碳税。这些税费会对碳排放强调较高和严重污染行业的资产产生负面影响，但同时会构成对低碳和清洁产业的市场利好。此外，企业若有破坏环境的行为或发生环境事故，也会使该企业和投资于这个企业的金融机构面临声誉风险和法律风险。

（二）环境风险分析方法

2016年和2017年的《综合报告》都强调了金融机构开展环境风险分析的必要性，2017年的《综合报告》及其背景报告还列举了十几个金融机构开展环境风险分析的案例。2017年9月，在

中国金融学会绿色金融委员会的指导下，工商银行主办了"金融业环境风险分析国际研讨会"，研讨了国际上多种环境压力测试、敏感性分析等方法，以及它们在银行、资管和保险业的运用。

总体来看，对金融机构和投资标的的环境风险分析还处于初级阶段，目前的已经见诸文献的方法包括环境压力测试、敏感性分析、ESG评分等。

1.对资产组合开展环境压力测试

资产管理业的环境压力测试是一种以定量分析为主的环境和气候风险分析方法。它通过模拟资产组合中的资产（如股票、债券、房产）在遇到环境和气候事件等压力情景下可能发生估值变化或违约率变化，测算环境和气候风险对资产组合的投资收益率的影响，分析环境和气候风险给投资可能带来的损失，从而帮助资管业减少或避免这些风险敞口。

中国工商银行开发了一套"压力测试"方法，用于评估环保政策变化对污染行业借款人的违约率的影响，这个方法可以为资产管理业所借鉴。中央财经大学绿色金融国际研究院对基金和保险资产管理业环境压力测试展开了研究。以沪深300指数为研究对象，这项研究结合敏感性分析与情景分析，探讨碳价风险、环保处罚风险和水资源风险对投资组合可能造成的收益率影响与减损风险值。

在研究能源结构变化以及相关政策可能产生的金融影响方面，机构投资者也已经积累了一些经验。比如，德盛安联资产管理公司与剑桥大学合作设计了一个模型，用于估算温室气体排放和能源政策对高排放企业盈利的影响。

2.敏感性分析

敏感性分析是通过模型分析找出环境因素变化与投资收益率之间的关系，如环境风险增加一

单位对于收益率或违约率的影响幅度。例如，敏感性分析可以用来估算碳价和水价上涨100%导致企业盈利下跌和股票估值下跌的百分比。对债券来说，敏感性分析可用于碳价、水价上涨和气候变暖等环境因素变化对债券违约率的影响。

3.ESG评分法

许多境外投资机构已经将ESG因素纳入其投资风险分析与决策中。一般认为，ESG得分较高的资产，环境风险就较低，因此以ESG为考虑因素之一的投资决策流程可以产生比较绿色的、环境风险较低的资产组合。有的资产管理公司会参考第三方机构如MSCI、Bloomberg提供的对各种资产（如上市公司和债券发行人）的ESG评级；也有的会自己设计一套ESG评估方法。比如，施罗德QEP投资团队的ESG投资策略是，在获取MSCI的ESG评级数据基础上，进一步对行业配置进行调整。

五、绿色投资的财务表现

近年来，越来越多的实证研究表明，绿色投资组合往往比非绿色投资和主流指数有更好的长期回报率。主要原因是，绿色投资组合剔除了环境和气候风险较大的标的（股票、债券等），因此减少了投资所面临的物理和转型因素导致的下行风险，从而可以提高长期回报率、降低波动率。下文综述部分关于环境和ESG表现与投资回报率关系的实证研究结果。

1.良好的环境绩效对股价有积极影响

Andreas Ziegler（2007）利用资产定价模型和多元回归模型分析了1996—2001年欧洲股票市场企业可持续发展绩效指标[1]与股票价格之间的关系，结果显示环境绩效对股价有积极影响[2]。

---

[1]可持续发展指标分为两个层面：一是公司所属行业的环境和社会风险；二是公司与行业内的其他公司相比，进行的环境和社会相关活动。

[2] 股票的月度收益率来衡量股东价值。

2.碳风险较低的股票表现较优

ET Index Research（2015）选取世界各国2267只股票作为样本进行实证研究，覆盖了全球最大的上市公司，代表了全球资本市场的85%。结果显示，在2008年到2015年，碳风险低[1]的股票的回报率显著优于碳风险高的股票。其中，供应链的碳风险[2]与股价的负相关关系最为明显。

Oestreich and Tsiakas（2015）就欧洲碳市场对德国不同行业的股票表现所产生的影响展开了实证分析。结果显示，需要购买碳配额的公司（即减排不努力的公司）的股价会受到碳风险的负面影响。

3. ESG优秀组合的表现优于市场基准

Nagy et al.（2016）发现，两个考虑了ESG因素的投资组合（分别为用ESG倾斜策略和ESG动量策略所建立相应投资组合）在2007年至2015年间的年均收益率均高于全球基准，采用ESG倾斜策略高于全球基准1.06%，采用ESG动量策略则

高于全球基准2.2%。

基于ESG倾斜策略[3]，Kumar et al.（2017）[4]运用静态与动态的ESG绩效指标对MSCI ACWI Index进行重新加权组合，进而建立了MSCI ESG Universal Index。模拟显示，该指数在2009年9月到2016年7月的年均收益率高出母指数20个基点，而风险溢价则降低了30个基点。

4. 中国绿色投资的收益明显

中央财经大学绿色金融国际研究院根据我国数据编制了"绿色领先股票指数"，该指数以沪深300股票为样本，采用定性、定量、企业负面环境新闻及环保处罚等指标进行筛选和排名。该指数在2011年11月至2016年6月回测年回报率表现优于沪深300指数近一倍，证明我国企业的绿色表现与股价呈高度正相关。此外，该研究还表明，越重视环境管理的企业，一般经营管理能力也越强，业绩表现越好。

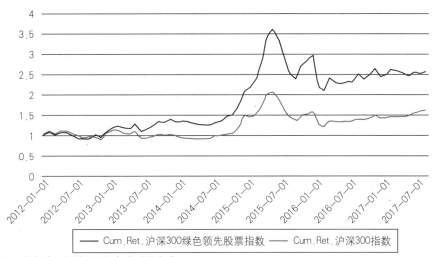

数据来源：中央财经大学国际绿色金融研究院。

图1　沪深300指数与沪深300绿色领先指数

[1] 该研究将公司的温室气体排放量，换算成二氧化碳计量，然后除以公司收入进行标准化处理。

[2] 碳排放核算分为三个范围：范围1是直接排放；范围2是购买电力的非直接排放；范围3是其他所有的非直接排放，包括供应链上下游的碳排放。

[3]ESG倾斜策略：追踪ESG整体表现稳健且未来趋势良好的，同时尽量缩小的排除范围。首先定义一个可投资的范围，排除一系列核心问题如参与武器相关行业和有违反国际规范的行为的企业；然后优化静态和动态的ESG表现因子来给剩下的股票加权，从而保持投资的多样化并平衡各种类型投资者的需求。

[4] Keep It Broad: An Approach to ESG Strategic Tilting.

商道融绿与兴全基金联合发布的《中国责任投资十年报告》显示，2014年8月至2017年8月期间，我国12只关注上市公司ESG绩效的指数在过去三年的表现明显优于沪深300和上证180等指数。波动率更低、夏普比率更高和平均收益率更高的指数分别有9只、10只和11只。这表明依据环境、社会和公司治理绩效进行筛选，所得到的投资组合财务回报较高，风险较低。

表2　ESG投资指数与样本空间指数绩效对比

指数简称	对比指数简称	夏普比率		波动率		平均收益率	
		指数/对比指数		指数/对比指数		指数/对比指数	
ESG 100	沪深300	0.211	0.173	8.708	8.527	2.089	1.725
ESG 40	180治理	0.188	0.168	9.275	9.416	1.997	1.829
180碳效	上证180	0.112	0.169	6.743	8.878	0.904	1.753
南方低碳	沪深300	0.232	0.173	8.204	8.527	2.152	1.725
责任指数	治理指数	0.2	0.17	8.592	9.094	1.973	1.797
深证责任	深证A指	0.222	0.157	7.931	10.072	2.007	1.829
中小责任	中小板指	0.217	0.12	8.744	9.647	2.151	1.412
180治理	上证180	0.168	0.169	9.416	8.878	1.829	1.753
治理指数	A股指数	0.17	0.151	9.094	8.264	1.797	1.5
巨潮治理	沪深300	0.246	0.173	7.484	8.527	2.092	1.725
深证治理	深证A指	0.253	0.157	7.883	10.072	2.244	1.829
中小治理	中小板指	0.174	0.12	9.109	9.647	1.834	1.412

数据来源：商道融绿；　注：红色表示指标高于对比项。

六、我国资产管理绿色化面临的问题与对策

（一）主要问题

我国资产管理的绿色化进程才刚刚开始，还存在很多问题和挑战，主要有以下几个方面：

1.环境风险管理和绿色投资意识较弱

目前多数国内机构投资者对环境相关的风险管理意识缺乏，对绿色投资并不理解。一些机构的高管对绿色投资原则还不了解，没有建立起相应的团队，没有投入足够的资源进行研究和产品开发。提供绿色投资决策咨询的券商研究机构和第三方机构也较少。

2.企业披露的环境信息有限

企业环境信息披露是资产管理公司开展分析环境风险和开展绿色投资的重要基础。目前市场普遍反映可用于环境因素分析的指标和信息较少，且缺乏可比性。例如由于缺少数据使得目前针对A股绿色策略的相关回测较少而且准确度有限。

3.缺乏绿色金融产品

截至2017年11月30日，国内基金管理机构已推出以环保、低碳、新能源、清洁能源、可持续、社会责任、环境治理为主题的绿色证券投资基金约103只，规模约812.81亿元。当前与成熟市场（尤其是欧洲）相比较，我国绿色投资产品占资本市场总规模的比例仍十分有限。绿色指数产

品、绿色资产证券化产品、绿色基金、绿色ABS以及绿色REIT等还无法满足日益增长的责任投资者的需求。

4.缺乏绿色风险分析能力

环境风险分析的理念、工具和方法在中国刚刚开始传播，研究和使用的机构还很少。我国的多数资产管理公司对环境风险分析的意义还不理解，有的甚至没有听说过这个概念。同时，由于这类工具和方法的使用者有限，尚未得到足够用户的检验，还有许多需要完善的地方。

（二）如何推动资管绿色化

针对以上问题，政府、行业协会、投资者应该共同在如下几个方面作出努力：

1.建立和完善上市公司强制性环境信息披露制度

金融市场是一个基于信息披露的市场，信息披露为资产的有效定价、为投资者识别投资机会与风险提供了主要依据。上市公司必须充分披露环境信息，投资者才能有效地识别绿色企业并向绿色企业配置资金。2016年12月，中国证监会正式发布修订公开发行证券的公司信息披露内容与格式准则，强制要求属于中国环境保护部门公布的重点排污单位的上市公司及其子公司在年度报告及半年度报告中进行环境信息披露。今后，证监会还要面向全部上市公司分三个阶段逐步建立强制性环境信息披露制度。目前已对属于环境保护部公布的重点排污单位的上市公司，制定了对主要污染物达标排放情况、企业环保设施建设和运行情况以及重大环境事件的具体信息披露要求。预计2018年监管部门将对其他上市公司的环境信息披露实行"不披露就解释"政策，2020年将强制要求所有上市公司披露环境信息。

2.宣传绿色投资可提升长期回报的理念

当前，国内许多资产管理机构的绿色投资意识还比较弱，普遍停留在绿色投资需要牺牲投资回报的认识上。但是，部分开展绿色投资的资产管理公司已经认识到，绿色投资的长期表现能够跑赢大市，也能帮助投资者规避环境风险。对这样的经验和研究结果，应该加大普及和宣传的力度。

3.政府背景的长期机构投资者应率先开展绿色投资

发展绿色金融是我国的国家战略，政府背景的长期机构投资者有义务率先开展绿色和责任投资。比如，主权投资机构、社保基金、国有保险公司等就应该率先配置绿色资产，率先开展ESG评级，率先进行环境风险分析，率先披露环境信息。从这些机构自身发展来看，开展绿色投资也有助于提升其经风险调整后的长期回报率。要充分认识到，大型投资者的绿色投资能支持经济的可持续发展，而经济的可持续发展反过来又会为这些机构获得长期回报提供基础。

4.鼓励绿色金融产品的开发

我国绿色证券指数化投资已取得了初步发展，目前已推出了21只绿色股票指数和7只绿色债券指数。此外，证监会还在积极研究碳排放权期货产品。但与成熟资本市场相比，中国资本市场上绿色证券产品较少、投资规模较小、投资者数量有限，需进一步推动绿色指数、绿色资产证券化、绿色基金等金融产品的开发与创新。

5.支持第三方机构对绿色资产评级和评估

当前许多资管公司对环境风险认识不足，分析能力有限。应该借助有经验的第三方评估机构对环境风险进行评估或对绿色企业进行评级，鼓励其充分利用企业披露的环境信息，并加工为ESG和绿色指数、绿色评级等产品。

6.强化环境风险分析等能力建设

我国监管机构和行业协会将支持绿色投资理念的推广，鼓励机构投资者发布绿色投资的责任报告，提升其对所投资产涉及的环境风险和碳排放的分析能力，就环境和气候因素的影响开展压力测试，保护绿色投资者利益。绿金委正组织

银行、基金、保险业开展环境压力测试和风险分析，不久将出版相关研究报告。

7.鼓励我国机构投资者披露环境信息

大型资产管理机构披露其投资组合的绿色或ESG表现，可以倒逼被投资企业强化环境信息披露。目前，绿金委正组织金融机构准备开展环境信息披露试点，初期可考虑对所持有的部分资产进行碳足迹和绿色化程度的评估和披露，中期应争取对所持有大部分资产的绿色化程度和环境影响进行披露。

8.鼓励我国机构投资者采纳责任投资原则

联合国责任投资原则组织（UNPRI）根据各国投资者的实践经验，总结了有关绿色投资的策略和方法，所提出的责任投资原则对我国有相当大的借鉴意义。加入这类国际平台，有助于我国资管机构充分借鉴国际经验、工具和方法，扩大我国绿色投资的国际影响力，也有助于我国资管业走出去，获得更多管理国际资本的机会。

参考文献：

[1] Harris J. The Emerging Importance of Carbon Emission-Intensities and Scope 3 （Supply Chain） Emissions in Equity Returns[J]. Social Science Electronic Publishing, 2015. Accessed at: https://www.etindex.com.

[2] Nagy Z, Kassam A, Lee L E. Can ESG Add Alpha? An Analysis of ESG Tilt and Momentum Strategies[J]. Journal of Investing, 2016, 25（2）:113-124.

[3] Oestreich A M, Tsiakas I. Carbon emissions and stock returns: Evidence from the EU Emissions Trading Scheme[J]. Journal of Banking & Finance, 2015, 58:294-308.

[4] Ziegler A, Schröder M, Rennings K. The effect of environmental and social performance on the stock performance of european corporations[J]. Environmental & Resource Economics, 2008, 40（4）:609.

[5] Neeraj K, Veronique M, Stuart D, Laura N，Keep It Broad: An Approach to ESG Strategic Tilting，2017.

Promoting the Greening of Asset Management in China

■ Ma Jun   Wang Junxian[1]

Abstract: The traditional task for asset managers was to obtain the best returns under the risk and restraints specified by investors, while taking no account of environmental factors. However, asset management greening has entered the mix in recent years. The asset management greening requires asset managers to take the environmental and social impacts posed by investments into consideration, both in the process of decision-making as well as in ROI-assessment（return on investment）. There through reducing investments in pollutants and high-carbon assets and increase the investment in clean and low-carbon assets.

The G20 Green Finance Study Group（GFSG）, initiated and co-hosted by China, explicitly indicates several trends for the development of green finance in the G20 Green Finance Synthesis Report（hereinafter referred to as *Synthesis Report*）in 2016, which include the greening of institutional investors. In recent years, rapid progress has been made in China' green finance industry. *The Guidelines for Establishing the Green Financial System* jointly released by seven ministries and commissions（People's Bank of China, China Securities Regulatory Commission, Ministry of Finance, National Development and Reform Commission, Ministry of Environmental Protection, China Banking Regulatory Commission and China Insurance Regulatory Commission）clearly stipulates that the institutional investors shall be guided to launch green investments and encouraged to carry out environmental risk analysis. These guidance opinions are gradually evolving into specific measures, methods and tools, which will exert a profound influence on markets in the future.

This article provides an in-depth exploration on various issues, including the background

---

[1] Ma Jun is Director of the Center for Finance and Development of Tsinghua University, Chair of the Green Finance Committee of China Society for Finance and Banking, and former chief economist of People's Bank of China Research Bureau. Wang Junxian is a researcher of China Institute of Finance and Capital Markets.

of greening of the asset management industry, green investment strategy, environmental risk management and environmental stress tests, and bring forward suggestions on relevant policies.

Ⅰ. Background of Asset Management Greening

At present, climate and environmental factors impose more restrictions on sustainable economic and social development, which leads to an urgent worldwide need to transform the existing economic development model featuring high pollution, high energy consumption, and high emission into a green and low-carbon economy. In order to cope with these challenges, governments introduce relevant policies successively and proactively advance economic transformation. Our research suggests that the existing development model results from a polluting and high-carbon industrial structure which is mainly caused by polluting investments. The deep-rooted causes of these polluting investments rest with a lack of incentive mechanisms to support green investments and the abolition of a series of system drawbacks that are restricting green investment.

China is launching incentive mechanisms to support green investment, which include re-lending from the central bank, interest subsidies, guarantees, and government funds. However, it is inadequate to boost investment greening only by virtue of incentive mechanisms formulated by the government in the context of limited fiscal capacity and enormous demand on green investment. The asset management industry administers

tremendous funds of private sectors. By the end of 2016, global institutional investors administer about 100 trillion dollars of assets. In China, institutional investors administer 116 trillion yuan of assets[1]. If the asset managers have no preference for green investment and over-invest in polluting and high-carbon assets, the transformation of economic greening can't be achieved. In other words, the asset management greening plays a key role in building green financial system.

The asset management greening requires that institutional investors take account of environmental factors in the process of investment decision-making. In some mature capital markets, green investment of asset management institutions resulted from accountability which requests assets managers to ensure the interests and claims of asset owners are fulfilled. Part of asset owners (e.g. religious funds and pension funds) propose claims to take climate and environmental factors into account, which forces asset managers to begin paying attention to green investments. For instance, Pensioenfonds Zorg en Welijin (PFZW) declares that its sustainable investment (green energy, clean technology, precautionary technology for water shortage etc.) will reach EURO 16 billion by 2020 decreasing the carbon footprint in the investment portfolio by 50%. In recent years, the concept of green investment has been strengthened on account of public opinion requirements, promotions by NGOs, as well as through the Paris Agreement, G20 initiatives, and other policies. In China, the promotion of green investment primarily relies on the government, e.g. "Two Mountains" Theory, *the Integrated Reform Plan for*

---

[1] The data is derived from Forward–looking Industry Research Institute.

Promoting Ecological Progress, the Guidelines for Establishing the Green Financial System and other policies and documents.

II. Principles for Responsible Investment (PRI)

Driven by the above-mentioned factors, more and more institutional investors begin to pay attention to principles for green and responsible investment. The *Synthesis Report* in 2016 puts forward that organizations can popularize and adopt UN Principles for Responsible Investment (PRI) and other green financial criteria on a voluntary basis as specific content for green finance development and reinforce the function for capacity building of PRI and other institutions.

PRI requires that institutional investors shall be expressly aware of environmental, social and corporate governance (ESG) issues and advocate them to fully take into consideration ESG factors in the process of investment decision-making. The term "green" in green finance refers to environmental factors, which is one of the factors responsible investments should consider. Responsible investments rely six specific principles:

1. Take account of environmental, social and corporate governance (ESG) factors in the process of investment analysis and decision-making;

2. Attach more importance to environmental, social and corporate governance (ESG) factors while exercising stockholder's rights;

3. Require invested institutions to disclose information on environmental, social and corporate governance (ESG);

4. Facilitate the investment industry to accept and implement principles for responsible investment;

5. Set up cooperative mechanisms and enhance implementation effect of PRI;

6. Disclose actions taken and progress made for implementing principles for responsible investment.

The principles for responsible investment were initiated in 2006 and the United Nations Principles for Responsible Investment (UNPRI) was established on this basis. The principles have been actively supported by a large number of institutional investors across the world since it was raised. In 2006, there were only 100 signatories of the principles for responsible investment around the globe with a total managed asset of 6.5 trillion dollars; while by June 2017, there were 1715 signatories with total managed asset of 62 trillion dollars. Most of signatories come from Europe (696) and the USA (256). The number of signatories from emerging market countries is growing rapidly. According to latest data, the number of signatories from Brazil, South Africa and China (including Hong Kong) are 57, 52 and 23 respectively[1]. The institutional investors signing up to the PRI are made up of many mainstream asset management institutions on a global scale, including Blackstone Group, CalPERS, Deutsche Asset & Wealth Management, Allianz SE, Old Mutual, Pension Fund of Banco do Brasil, Japan's Government Pension Investment Fund (GPIF), South Korea's National Pension Service and Canada Pension Plan (CPP) as well as China Asset Management Co., Ltd. and E Fund Management Co., Ltd.

---

[1] See www.unpri.org.

In addition, the Portfolio Decarbonisation Coalition （PDC） is co-launched by the United Nations Environment Programme Finance Initiative （UNEP FI） with PRI as its supporting unit. The PDC consists of 27 large-scale institutional investors that pursue low carbon objectives, including The Fourth Swedish National Pension Fund （AP4）, Amundi Asset Management and BNP Paribas Asset Management. PDC advocates investors to take systematic approaches in an attempt to make investment portfolios meet low carbon requirements. Those systematic approaches contain the following aspects: （1） Reduce carbon footprint of investment portfolio. （2） Increase the investments in renewable energy （3） Disinvest from energy-intensive activities. （4） Encourage invested enterprises to reduce carbon emissions and. （5） Support low-carbon economic transformation. According to PDC annual report in 2016, all of the 27-member institutions have vigorously taken measures to reduce carbon footprint in investment portfolio, among which 17 institutions that have disclosed carbon footprint index for part or all of their investment portfolios.

In China, the Green Finance Committee of China Society for Finance and Banking （GFC）, the Asset Management Association of China, and the China Institute of Finance and Capital Markets etc. collaborated with the United Nations Principles for Responsible Investment （UNPRI） to carry out a training activity regarding responsible investment for domestic institutional investors for the first time in July 2016. More than 60 institutional investors participated in the training activity. Afterwards, multiple seminars on this issue were held. Over the past few years, the China Social Investment Forum jointly held by the GFC and SYNTAO in collaboration with

various institutions has constantly advanced principles, tools and methods for responsible investment.

III. Investment Strategy for Green Asset Management

PRI proposes a series of basic principles for promotion of green and responsible investment in terms of the relationship between asset owners and asset management institutions as well as the readership between asset management institutions and investees. In the process of specific asset management work, in aspects of investment strategy and method, what changes does a chief investment officer （CIO）, a chief risk officer （CRO）, and a fund manager in an asset management institution need to make? On the basis of international experience, institutional investors mainly implement green investment by the following seven types of investment strategies and methods:

（ i ） Blacklist mechanism

Blacklist mechanism means excluding the investments with relatively high environmental risks or ESG risks, such as setting some standards at the moment of making investment decisions and excluding the stocks or securities of polluting or high-carbon enterprises from optional investment targets. For instance, APG Asset Management of the Netherlands has excluded all the petrochemical stocks from its investment portfolio and Allianz SE has cancelled the investment for coal industry.

（ ii ） Whitelist mechanism

Whitelist mechanism means selecting the industry and companies with excellent environmental performance to invest. For instance, Pensioenfonds Zorg en Welijn （PFZW） has selected those enterprises which deliver best outcomes of carbon emission reduction in several industries, including green energy, clean technology, food safety and water resources. What's more, AEGON-INDUSTRIAL Fund has established a green stock pool and an overall rating and ranking are determined for each enterprise according to the performance on environmental responsibility, thus selecting outstanding enterprises to invest.

（iii） ESG strategy

ESG strategy means adding environmental or ESG factors based on the existing investment strategy. For example, asset management companies can add ESG rating indexes （a large number of rating indexes can be obtained from Bloomberg or MSCI） based on existing models and methods for asset allocation or selection to make asset allocation or selection results for stocks and securities greener.

（iv） Green index investment

Green index investment refers to passive investment in several green index products, including low carbon index, new energy index, ESG index and environmental protection index. Currently, there are hundreds of green indexes around the globe and the famous ones include S&P eco-index and MSCI environmental index. Domestically, there are 21 green stock indexes and 16 green security indexes, some of which has been utilized as fund products. For instance, the tracking target for Securities Investment Fund of Fortis CSI China Mainland Low Carbon Economy Index is CSI China Mainland Low Carbon Economy Index, and Classification Securities

Investment Fund of BOCOM Schroders CNI New Energy Index tracks CNI New Energy Index.

（v） Green-themed investment

Green-themed investment means investing in one or several kinds of entities or industries related to environmental conscience business practices. For instance, multiple institutions launch green building funds, clean energy funds, environmental protection funds dedicated to sewage treatment, etc. Denmark pension fund ATP has invested in equity and credits of enterprises associated with renewable resources and clean energy sectors and contributed EURO 1 billion to climate change funds as a way to invest in emerging market countries. Hybrid securities investment funds based on clean energy strives to achieve long-term and sustainable growth on the premise of rationally controlling risk and maintaining strong liquidity of fund assets by meticulously selecting relevant securities invested in funds themed in clean energy.

（vi） Social impact investment

Social impact investment refers to the investment which endeavours to obtain environmental and social benefits while pursuing financial returns. This sort of fund investment mainly targets environmental protection, environmental change response, poverty alleviation, education etc. Some of this investment is also known as social enterprises which call for re-investing most of its profits in social and environmental public welfare programs. At the moment, most organizations taking part in this kind of investment are family charitable foundations and pensions and other social capital is gradually being added.

（vii）Shareholders engagement

Institutional investors are authorized to execute shareholders' rights representing asset owners, thus affecting environmental and social performance of invested enterprises. For instance, shareholders can exercise rights on the corporate environmental issues at general shareholders meeting to urge enterprises to lay more emphasis on environmental responsibility and information disclosure. They are also entitled to communicate with corporate executives and ask the company for more participation in green investment and a reduction of polluting activities. For example, Hermes Fund Management that administers more than 10 billion dollars has earned long-term financial returns by means of bringing positive influence on ESG performance to their invested enterprises[1].

According to the data from the Global Sustainable Investment Alliance（GSIA for short）1, the total amount of green and responsible investment worldwide has reached about 22.9 trillion dollars as of 2016, rising by 25% compared with 2014. This kind of investment accounts for 26% of global investments. At present, the USA, Canada and Europe stands out in in the international markets while Japan, Australia and New Zealand are growing rapidly. The investment strategy with the largest proportion of actors in the world is the blacklist mechanism, followed by the integrated ESG strategy. Asian countries besides Japan have recoded slow growth in overall market of responsible investment, with total asset scale reaching 52.1 billion dollars in 2016.

As per the data statistics from the Wind system database, the current scale of green and responsible investment in Chinese asset management has reached 12.3 billion dollars （note: this figure is incomparable with GSIA data in that the statistical calibers vary among different countries）. Although comparable statistics are not available yet, researches show that there are a few institutional investors involved in green and responsible investments in China. On the one hand, a huge gap persists between China and international frontiers （especially Europe）; on the other hand, Chinese green and responsible investment market enjoys enormous potential for development.

Table 1 Global green and responsible investment （2016）

Unit: One billion dollars

Region	Total assets	Ratio of total investment in the region	Ratio of total global green and responsible investment
EU	12040	52.6%	52.6%
USA	8723	21.6%	38.1%
Canada	1086	37.8%	4.7%
Australia & New Zealand	516	50.6%	2.3%
Asia （excluding Japan）	52	0.8%	0.2%
Japan	474	3.4%	2.1%

Data source: GSIA.

---

[1] See GSIA Global Sustainable Investment Report in 2016.

IV. Environmental Risk Analysis and Management

Environmental risk analysis and management is the main vehicle for green investing in the asset management industry. Effective identification and management of environmental risks is beneficial for asset management companies to mitigate downward risks caused by environmental factors, including stock valuation decline and bond default. Hence, a long-term rate of return for investment portfolio can be delivered. Risk analysis holds the comprehensive（macroscopic）significance to drive the financial sector to reduce the investment allocation on polluting and high-carbon industry and increase allocation on green industry.

（i）Risk classification

In 2017, the G20 Green Finance Study Group indicate two main kinds of environmental risks confronted by financial market, namely physical environmental risk and transformation-related environmental risks.

1. Physical risk:

Physical risk refers to the destructive impact on human and economic activities caused by pollution and climate change. These risks derive from air pollution, water pollution, soil pollution, natural disaster, climate change, water resources shortage, natural capital degradation, etc. Climate change is closely connected with various natural disasters as it can dramatically increase the frequency of the these.

Many industries, including agriculture, mining, tourism and ocean-going fishing, are greatly influenced by climate risks（e.g. flood, drought, hurricane and typhoon）. There are numerous incidents that can influence many industries and enterprises, such as sea level rise, global warming as well as unexpected water and soil pollution. These risks might result in declining enterprise capacity, rising cost, labor shortage, premature fixed asset retirement, damaged buildings, and faltering demand.

2. Transformation risk:

Transformation risk refers to the risk mainly caused by human factors, which include change of policy and regulation, rising prices of carbon（due to government quotas reduction）, technical change and reputational loss. For instance, high emission enterprises are encountered when risks such as uplifted environmental fines, increased cost for carbon quota purchases, which may lead to profit shrinkage, valuation decrease and default rate rise. Some governments will increase taxes on pollutant emission or levy taxes on carbon. These taxes will exert adverse impact on the assets of highly-intensive carbon emission and heavily-polluting industries, while they can also create a bullish market for low-carbon and purification industries. In the event that an enterprise conducts itself in a manner impeding to the deterioration of the environment or causes an environmental accident, this enterprise will put itself and the financial institution that invest in it at financial, reputational, and legal risk.

（ii）Method for environmental risk analysis

The *Synthesis Report* in 2016 and 2017 both stress the necessity of financing institutions to carry out environmental risk analysis. The *Synthesis Report* in 2017 and its background report also list a dozen of cases on how financial institutions carry out

risk assessments. In September 2017, under the guidance of Green Finance Committee of China Society for Finance and Banking （GFC）, the Industrial and Commercial Bank of China has launched the "the international seminar of environmental risk analysis in the financial industry" where participants discus on several methods for environmental stress tests and sensitivity analysis, and their application in banking, asset management and insurance industries.

In general, the environmental risk analysis for financial institutions and investment targets are still preliminary, and methods published on the literature include environmental stress tests, sensitivity analysis, ESG grading, etc.

1. Conduct environmental stress tests for asset portfolio

Environmental stress testing in the asset management industry is a kind of environment and climate risk analysis method centred on quantitative analysis. Through simulating the change of assessed value or default rate of assets （like stock, bond, house property） in an asset portfolio under stresses like environmental and climatic events, measuring the impact of environmental and climatic risk on return on investment of asset portfolio, and analyzing the potential losses caused by environmental and climatic risk on investment, the environmental stress test helps the asset management industry reduce or avoid these risks exposure.

The Industrial and Commercial Bank of China has developed a set of "stress test" methods to evaluate the impact of changes of environmental policies on default rate of borrowers in the pollution industry, which may be used for reference by the asset management industry.

The International Institute of Green Finance, Central University of Finance and Economics has carried out research on the environmental stress tests against fund and insurance asset management industries. With the CSI 300 index as the object, this research explored the potential impact of a carbon price risk, environmental penalty risks and risk of water resources on the rate of return of the investment portfolio and the impairment risk value associated with different scenarios.

While researching the impact of changes of energy mix and relevant policies on finance, the institutional investors have also accumulated certain experience. For example, Allianz Global Investors and University of Cambridge have designed a model together, to estimate the impact of greenhouse gas emission and energy policy on the profit of enterprises with heavy emission.

2. Sensitivity analysis

Sensitivity analysis has looked at the relation between changes of environmental factors and returns on investment through model analysis. I.e. the range of effect of the addition of one unit environmental risk on the rate of return or default rate. For example, the sensitivity analysis may be used to estimate the percentage of enterprise earnings drop/ stock valuation drop caused by 100% rising of carbon and water price. The sensitivity analysis may be used to measure the impact of the changes of environmental factors like carbon and water price rising and climate warming on bond default rate.

3. ESG point system

Many overseas investment organizations have included ESG factors into their investment risk analysis and decision. It is generally recognized that the higher the ESG points, the lower the environmental risk. Therefore, the decision-making procedure with ESG as one of the factors may generate green asset portfolios with relatively low environmental risk. Some assets management companies may refer to the ESG grading of various assets （like listed company and the issuing of bonds） provided by MSCI, Bloomberg and other third-party organizations, while others design a set of ESG evaluation method by themselves. For example, the ESG investment strategy of Schroder QEP investment team is further adjusting the industry distribution on the basis of obtaining MSCI and ESG grading data.

V. Financial Performance of Green Investment

In recent years, more and more empirical researches show that green investment portfolio enjoys better long-term rate of return when compared with non-green investment and the index of the mainstream. The main reason is that the green investment portfolio evades some degree of environment and climate risks （stock, bond, etc）, thereby reducing the downside risk caused by the physical and transitional factors facing the investment, and improving the long-term rate of return & reducing the volatility. The following text summarizes the result of empirical study of relation between environment or ESG

performance and rate of return.

1. Positive influence of favorable environmental performance on share price

Andreas Ziegler （2007） analyzes enterprise sustainable development performance indicators[1] of European stock market in 1996-2001 by using asset pricing model and multiple regression models, and the result shows that the environmental performance exerts positive effects on the share price[2].

2. The performance of stock with lower carbon risk is superior

ET Index Research （2015） conducts an empirical study by selecting 2267 stocks from the world as the sample, covering the globally largest listed company and representing 85% of global capital market. The result show that the rate of return of the stock with low carbon risk[3] is superior to that with high carbon risk between 2008 and 2015, among which, the negative correlation between carbon risk[4] of supply chain and share price is the most obvious.

Oestreich and Tsiakas （2015） have launched an empirical analysis on the impact of European carbon market on stocks in different industries in Germany. The result shows that the share price of the companies （those not trying to cut emissions） needing to purchase carbon quota will be negatively impacted by the carbon risk.

[1] The sustainable development indicators are divided into two layers: 1） the environment and social risks in the industry where the company belongs; 2） compared with other companies in the industry, the environmental and social activities launched.

[2] The monthly rate of return of the stock will be used to measure the shareholder value.

[3] The research coverts the greenhouse gas emissions of the company to carbon dioxide, and then divides the company's income for standardized processing.

[4] The carbon emission accounting is divided into three ranges: range 1: direct emission; range 2: indirect emission of purchased electricity; range 3: indirect emission of others, including carbon emission in upstream and downstream of supply chains.

3. The performance of ESG excellent portfolio is superior to that of the market benchmark

Nagy et al. （2016） finds that the average annual return of two investment portfolios （relevant investment portfolios established with ESG tilting strategy and ESG momentum strategy） considering ESG factors is higher than that of the global benchmark between 2007-2015. The one adopting ESG tilting strategy is 1.06% higher than that of the global benchmark, and the one adopting ESG momentum strategy is 2.2% higher than that of the global benchmark.

Based on the ESG tilting strategy[1], Kumar et al. （2017） applies static and dynamic ESG performance indicators to conduct weighted array again for MSCI ACWI Index, and thus to establish MSCI ESG Universal Index. The analog displays that the average annual return of the index from September 2009 to July 2016 is 20 base points higher than the benchmark index, while the risk premium is reduced by 30 base points.

4. The earnings of China green investment are obvious

The International Institute of Green Finance, Central University of Finance and Economics developed the "green leading stock index" in light of the data of China, which adopts CSI 300 stock as the sample, as well as qualitative indexes and quantitative indexes, corporate negative environmental news and environmental penalties and other indexes for screening and ranking. The performance rate of return for this index from November 2011 to June 2016 is superior to CSI 300 index, at nearly twice the growth rate, certifying that the green performance of our enterprises is highly positively correlated with the share price. In addition, the research also shows that enterprises boast stronger operating and management capability and better performance if they attach importance to environmental management.

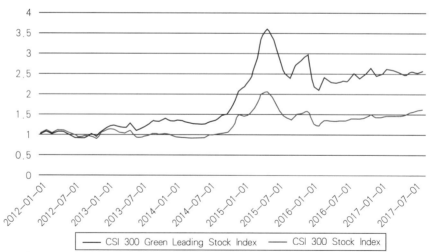

Data source: International Institute of Green Finance, Central University of Finance and Economics

Figure1   SCI 300 stock index and CSI 300 green leading stock index

---

[1] ESG tilting strategy: Track and ensure that the overall performance of ESG is robust and promising, and try to narrow the range of exclusion. Firstly, define the scope of investment, and exclude a series of core issues, like joining in weapon-relevant industry, or violating international norms; then optimize the static and dynamic ESG performance factors for the remaining stock weighting, and thus keep the diversification of investment and balance the demands of each kind of investors.

SynTao Green Finance and AEGON-Industrial Fund issued *A Decade's Report of China's Responsible Investment*, which shows that the performance of 12 indexes focusing on the ESG performance of listed company is superior to indexes of CSI 300 and SSE 180 in the past three years from August 2014 to August 2017. There are 9, 10 and 11 indexes with lower volatility, higher Sharpe ratio and higher average rate of return, respectively. This shows that the financial returns of the investment portfolio are higher and the risks are lower when screened as per the environment, society and performance of corporate governance.

Table 2　Comparison of performance of ESG investment index and sample space index

Index abbreviation	Comparative index abbreviation	Sharpe ratio index/ comparative index		Volatility index/ comparative index		Average rate of return index/ comparative index	
ESG 100	CSI 300	0.211	0.173	8.708	8.527	2.089	1.725
ESG 40	180 Governance	0.188	0.168	9.275	9.416	1.997	1.829
180 Carbon effect	Shanghai 180	0.112	0.169	6.743	8.878	0.904	1.753
Southern low carbon	Hushen 300	0.232	0.173	8.204	8.527	2.152	1.725
Responsibility index	Governance index	0.2	0.17	8.592	9.094	1.973	1.797
Shenzhen responsibility	Shenzhen A—index	0.222	0.157	7.931	10.072	2.007	1.829
Small and medium duty	SSE SME COMPOSITE	0.217	0.12	8.744	9.647	2.151	1.412
180 Governance	Shanghai 180	0.168	0.169	9.416	8.878	1.829	1.753
Governance index	A—share index	0.17	0.151	9.094	8.264	1.797	1.5
Juchao governance	Hushen 300	0.246	0.173	7.484	8.527	2.092	1.725
Shenzhen governance	Shenzhen A—index	0.253	0.157	7.883	10.072	2.244	1.829
Small and medium governance	SSE SME COMPOSITE	0.174	0.12	9.109	9.647	1.834	1.412

Data source: SynTao Green Finance; Note: Red indicates that the index is higher than the comparative item.

Ⅵ. Problems Facing China's Asset Management Greening and the Countermeasures

(ⅰ) Main problems

The development of China's asset management greening is just starting and there are many problems and challenges, such as the following aspects:

1. The awareness on environmental risk management and green investment is weak

Many domestic institutional investors lack awareness on environment-related risk management, and they do not know enough about green investment cases. Executives of some organizations know little about the

principles of green investment. They haven't established the correct team, or invested enough resources in research and product development. In addition, there are relatively few security research organizations and third-party organizations providing green investment policy-making consulting.

2. Environmental message disclosed by enterprises is limited

Enterprise environmental information disclosure serves as the important foundation for assets management companies to analyse environmental risks and launch green investments. Currently, there are few indexes and information for factoring environmental risks in the market. For example, the back-test on A-share green strategy has low accuracy due to a lack of data.

3. Lack of green products

As of November 30, 2017, the domestic fund management organizations have launched about 103 green security investment funds with environmental protection, low carbon, new energy, clean energy, sustainability, social responsibility and environmental governance as the subjects, at a total worth of 81.281 billion yuan. Compared with mature markets （especially the European market）, our green investment products account for a extremely limited share of the total capital market. Green index products, green asset securitization products, green funds, green ABS and green REIT still fail to meet the increasing requirement of the responsible investor.

4. Lack green risk analysis ability

Since the concept, tool and method of environmental risk are just spreading in China, there are few organizations researching on and applying it. Many assets management companies in China do not know much about the meaning of the environmental risk analysis, and some have not even heard about it. At the meantime, there are limited users of this kind of tools and methods, so we have not obtained enough user experience. There is ample much room for spreading research and practice.

（ii）How to promote asset management greening

In light of the issues above, we provide the government, industrial associations and investors with the following recommendations:

1. Establish and complete the mandatory environmental information disclosure system of listed companies

The financial market is based on information disclosure, which provides the main bases for the effective pricing of assets and identifies investment opportunity and risk for investors. The listed companies must fully disclose the environmental information, so that the investors may effectively identify green enterprises and deploy funds for green enterprises. In December 2016, China Securities Regulatory Commission formally issued the amended guidelines for content and format of company information disclosure of the publicly issued securities, compulsively requiring the listed companies and their subsidiaries of the key pollutant emission units published by China's environmental protection department to disclose the environmental information disclosure in the annual report and semi-annual report.

From now on, the China Securities Regulatory Commission will establish mandatory environment information disclosure system in three steps for all listed companies. Currently, the specific information disclosure requirements of key pollutant emission under certain standard, enterprise environmental protection facility construction and operation and other major environmental events are developed for the listed companies of the key pollutant emission units published by China's environmental protection department. It is expected that the supervision department will implement the policy of "explaining without disclosure" for environmental information disclosure of other listed companies. In 2020, all listed companies will be compulsively required to disclose environment information.

2. Disseminate the idea that green investment may increase long-term returns

Currently, many asset management organizations lack awareness of green investment. Generally, they omay think that the return of investment will be compromised in a green investment. However, asset management companies, which have launched green investments schemes, have realized that the long-term performance of green investment may be better than the market average, and also help investors evade environmental risks. This kind of experience- and research results shall be heavily popularized and publicized.

3. Government-related long-term institutional investors shall take the initiative to launch green investment

Developing green finance is a national strategy in China. Government-related long-term institutional investors shall take the initiative to launch green and responsible investments. For example, sovereign investors, social insurance funds, state-owned insurance companies shall act as the pioneers to allocate green assets, to carry out ESG grading, environment risk analysis, and to disclose environment information.

Seen from the development of these origins, launching green investment is also conducive to increasing the long-term rate of return after adjustment of risk. It must be fully recognized that large-scale green investment by investors may support the sustainable development of the economy, which in turn provides the basis for these organizations to obtain long-term return.

4. Encourage the development of green financial products

Our green security indexation investment has achieved impressive initial development. Currently, there are 21 green stock indexes and 7 green bond indexes. Besides, China Securities Regulatory Commission is actively researching on future products of carbon emission permit. However, compared with the mature capital market, Chinese capital market suffers less green security products, a small investment scale, and limited investment amount, therefore, efforts shall be made to promote the development and innovation of financial products like green index, green asset securitization, green funds, etc.

5.Render support to the third-party organizations to grade and evaluate the green assets

Many asset management companies are currently lacking awareness on environmental risks and subsequently their ability to carry out analysis is limited. Experienced third-party appraisal agencies shall be resorted to evaluate the environmental risk or grade the green enterprise, encouraging them to make the best use of the environment information disclosed by enterprises and process it to products like ESG and green index, green grading, etc.

6. Strengthen capacity building like environmental risk analysis

China's supervision organizations and industrial associations will support the promotion of green investment concepts, encourage the institutional investors to issue the responsibility report on green investment, and improve the analytical ability on environmental risk and carbon emission involved in the invested asset. Besides, the institutional investors are urged to carry out pressure test on impact of environmental and climate factors to protect the interests of green investors. The Green Finance Committee of the China Society of Financing and Banking is organizing banks, funds and insurance industries to carry out environmental stress test and risk analysis, and relevant research report will be published before long.

7. Encourage our institutional investors to disclose environment information

When large asset management organizations disclose green or ESG performance information of their investment portfolio, the invested enterprises are forced to strengthen the disclosure of environment information. Currently, the Green Finance Committee of China Society of Financing and Banking is organizing financial institutions to prepare for the pilot work of environment information disclosure. At the initial stage, they shall consider evaluation and disclosure on carbon footprint and the degree of greening for any assets they hold; during the medium term, they shall try to disclose the greening degree and environmental influence for most assets they hold.

8. Encourage our institutional investors to adopt the principle for responsible investment

United Nations' Principles for Responsible Investment (UNPRI) summarizes the strategies and methods on green investment in light of the practical experience of investors of various countries, and the principle for responsible investment proposed by it is of great referential value for China. Joining this kind of international platform can help asset management organizations to make the best use of international experiences, tools and methods, expand our international influence of green investments, and help China go global to obtain more opportunities for managing international assets.

References:

[1] Harris J. The Emerging Importance of Carbon Emission-Intensities and Scope 3 (Supply Chain) Emissions in Equity Returns[J]. Social Science Electronic Publishing, 2015. Accessed at: https://www.etindex.com.

[2] Nagy Z, Kassam A, Lee L E. Can ESG Add Alpha? An Analysis of ESG Tilt and Momentum Strategies [J]. Journal of Investing, 2016, 25 (2) :113-124.

[3] Oestreich A M, Tsiakas I. Carbon emissions and stock returns: Evidence from the EU Emissions Trading Scheme[J]. Journal of Banking & Finance, 2015, 58:294-308.

[4] Ziegler A, Schröder M, Rennings K. The effect of environmental and social performance on the stock performance of european corporations[J]. Environmental & Resource Economics, 2008, 40 (4) :609.

[5] Neeraj K, Veronique M, Stuart D, Laura N, Keep It Broad: An Approach to ESG Strategic Tilting, 2017.

中国绿色金融发展趋势展望及银行业在其中的作用

■ 周月秋[1]

摘要：习近平总书记在十九大报告中提到要 "加快生态文明体制改革"，"发展绿色金融"，这释放出了明确的政策信号，表明未来我国绿色金融将进入加速发展时期。绿色金融市场将更加完善和透明，全社会认同和倡导的绿色文化有望形成，我国在全球治理中也将发挥更加重要的作用。中国银行业将在资金支持、先行经验、工具和方法等多领域为我国及全球绿色金融发展贡献力量。

关键词：十九大　绿色金融　全球治理　银行业

习近平总书记在十九大报告中指出要"加快生态文明体制改革，建设美丽中国"，并将"发展绿色金融"定位为推进经济绿色发展的重要途径，这彰显了我国在改善环境、实现可持续发展问题上的决心和信念，巩固了绿色金融在生态文明建设中的战略性地位，表明中国绿色金融将迎来发展的"黄金时期"，并将继续在全世界发挥引领作用。

一、中国绿色金融发展现状

与发达国家开展的实践相比，中国绿色金融起步或许不是最早的，但旗帜鲜明、系统化地提出绿色金融并加以实施恐怕应该是最早的，发展速度一定是最快的，影响力也是最大的，在短短几年时间取得多项世界领先，完全可以说是创造了绿色金融领域的历史。

第一，中国是世界上拥有最完备绿色金融顶层设计的国家。十九大报告等党和国家的重要纲领性文件中都将绿色金融放在重要位置；2016年8月，七部委联合发布的《关于构建绿色金融体系的指导意见》是全球首个发展绿色金融的国家层面政策文件；2017年6月，我国启动了在浙江、江西、广东、贵州和新疆五省（自治区）建

---

[1] 周月秋系中国工商银行城市金融研究所所长。

设绿色金融改革创新试验区，标志着我国绿色金融已经进入创新实践的落地阶段。

第二，中国的绿色金融市场迅速发展。绿色信贷规模持续增长，对环境效益贡献显著；绿色债券市场爆发式增长，实现从零到全球第一的跨越式发展；全国统一的碳金融市场即将启动，成为中国应对全球气候变化的重要贡献之一；绿色产业发展基金、绿色保险、绿色信托等产品也开始加速发展。

第三，中国在担任2016年20国集团（G20）轮值主席国期间，首次将绿色金融列为G20核心议题，并得到了G20各国的一致支持，并直接影响到2017年德国G20和2018年阿根廷G20延续对绿色金融议题的关注。

二、十九大后中国绿色金融发展趋势

（一）中国将通过绿色金融在全球治理中发挥更重要作用

中国是全球第二大经济体，也是全球温室气体排放大国，中国以强烈的责任和担当在应对气候变化、保护地球环境方面做出积极贡献。近年来，中国系统地推进绿色金融制度建设、市场拓展及工具创新，全面促进经济可持续发展及转型，为G20新兴市场和发展中国家提供了重要示范。习近平总书记指出，未来中国将继续致力于构建人类命运共同体，"坚持环境友好"，建设"清洁美丽的世界"，"保护好人类赖以生存的地球家园"。在这一宏伟目标的指引下，未来绿色金融将在中国继续得到政府和社会各方面力量的支持，中国在全球绿色金融领域的领导力也将会不断增强。

我国可望从两个方面通过绿色金融积极参与全球治理：一方面，提升绿色金融中国标准的国际化建设，让中国标准成为世界标准。例如我国的绿色信贷指标体系，在银行业已经推行多

年，部分周边国家也开始参照我国经验构建其自身的指标体系，已经具备向全球推广的基础。此外，在环境信息披露标准建立方面，目前全球各国在这一领域的实践并不多，我国完全有可能实现突破。另一方面，通过绿色金融引领"一带一路"建设。绿色金融能够为"一带一路"建设提供资金、产品和信息的支持，降低环境风险，提供投融资标准，因此，发展"一带一路"，绿色金融不能缺位。同时，借助"一带一路"构建的全球联通平台，中国绿色金融也有望在推动全球经济复苏、应对气候变化等方面发挥更加重要的作用。

（二）中国绿色金融体系将更加完善和透明

在顶层设计的指引下，我国绿色金融体系的建设将日臻完善：绿色信贷市场将稳健发展，为绿色企业和项目持续提供便捷、低成本的融资；绿色债券市场将结束前期的超高速增长，进入稳定增长阶段，受到较低融资成本的鼓舞，企业和金融机构发行绿债（尤其是海外绿债）的步伐有望加速；碳市场将走向规范和统一，由此衍生出的期货交易，将成为地方绿色金融发展的亮点；绿色指数等量化产品和工具也将日趋丰富，引领责任投资走向主流。

此外，上市公司和发债企业环境信息强制披露机制有望建立，一个更加公平、公开、透明的市场使企业的正确定价成为可能。同时，在全球各国环境信息披露实践较少的背景下，我国信息披露机制有望成为"国际机制"。

（三）"市场驱动"在未来将发挥更加重要的作用

在前期政策拉动以及监管、执法的推动下，中国各类市场主体关注生态环境的内在动力逐步形成，具备生态发展的大环境，下一阶段，"市场动力"将逐渐取代"绿色情怀"，在未来中国

绿色金融的发展中发挥更加重要的作用。

首先，金融机构已经开始将环境因素纳入资本定价的考量因素中，这不仅是金融机构践行社会责任的需要，更是为了防范面临的环境与社会风险以及寻找新的业务增长点而做出的战略选择。例如，商业银行正在逐步压降和退出高污染、高能耗行业，将资金重点投放在环境友好、资源节约型的企业和项目中，未来污染环境的企业和项目将会很难从银行获得贷款，同时，由于绿色金融的系统化布局，从其他渠道获得融资支持的难度也会同步加大。其次，如果说"融资难""融资贵"是整个融资市场的现实，那么，污染企业将面对的是更加严苛的融资环境和压力，将不得不更加主动地进行经营转型和设备升级，从而将使环保企业投资回报率和盈利水平有所上升，而融资成本则呈现下降趋势，在正向激励的作用下，企业将更加积极地参与到绿色金融市场中。最后，在"五省试点"推动下，地方经济将从绿色金融发展中受益，全国各省纷纷布局绿色金融，特色化和个性化的发展模式以及创新型产品和服务也将陆续出现，地方绿色金融市场的探索将为全国绿色金融发展提供经验，这是对我国"自上而下"发展模式的重要补充。

（四）全社会认同和倡导的绿色文化有望形成

建设美丽中国不仅需要政府、企业和金融机构的努力，更需要在全社会形成统一的绿色发展价值观。十九大报告中强调"人与自然是生命共同体"，"要建设人与自然和谐共生的现代化"，倡导全民共同参与、共同治理环境。十九大后，绿色发展将更加深入人心，并成为全民关注和努力的重要方向。在资本市场中，ESG（环境、社会、公司治理）投资已经受到越来越多投资者的认可，除财务绩效外，企业的环境表现、社会形象已成为投资者为企业定价时考虑的重要因素。同时，我们还欣喜地看到，绿色金融已经

开始走入大学校园和课堂，中央财经大学和中国人民大学已经开设绿色金融方向的硕士专业和课程，这将对塑造我国新一代的绿色金融价值观、培养更多专业的绿色金融人才产生积极影响。

三、中国银行业是推动绿色金融发展的中流砥柱

（一）银行业为绿色融资提供资金支持

银行业是我国融资市场中最大的资金供给方，长期以来为支持实体经济建设，促进全国经济结构可持续转型提供了大量资金支持，必然也是绿色融资市场中最大的资金供给方。截至2017年2月末，国内21家主要银行机构绿色信贷余额达7.5万亿元，占各项贷款的9.0%，预计可年节约标准煤1.93亿吨，减排二氧化碳当量4.49亿吨，减排化学需氧量410.86万吨、氨氮44.88万吨、二氧化硫412.83万吨、氮氧化物207.22万吨，节水6.44亿吨。

随着生态文明建设战略的持续深入推进，发展绿色产业所需要的资金规模也在不断增加，银行业应当积极创新融资模式，开拓融资渠道，提升融资能力，持续为我国经济的绿色发展贡献力量。近两年，我国绿色债券市场发展迅速，受到国际投资者的高度关注，我国商业银行也纷纷启动海外绿色债券发行，为境外资金支持我国绿色产业建设搭建了桥梁，各大银行都在这一领域积极实践。特别值得一提的是，工商银行于2017年9月28日在卢森堡发行首只"一带一路"绿色气候债券，募集资金合计21.5亿美元，其中3年期欧元及美元两个发行品种中，欧洲投资者占有率均超过70%。这笔绿色债券的募集资金将用于支持工商银行已经投放或即将投放的可再生能源、低碳及低排放交通、能源效率和可持续水资源管理四类合格绿色信贷项目。

这次发行的绿债利率点差也处于中资可比

同业的最好水平，同时创下了多个市场纪录，包括第一笔同时满足国际和国内最新绿色债券标准的债券；第一笔获得国际气候与环境研究中心（CICERO）第二意见的中资机构绿色债券，并获得迄今为止唯一一个"深绿"最高评价；第一笔获得气候债券倡议组织（CBI）认证的中资金融机构债券；第一笔以"一带一路"沿线绿色项目为主题的绿色债券；同时还创造了单笔发行欧元金额最大的中资绿色债券纪录。

（二）银行业为绿色金融发展提供先行经验

首先，我国银行业金融机构在多年经营和管理绿色信贷的过程中，积累了大量实践经验，绿色信贷相关的政策和制度也能够为我国健全绿色金融系统提供参考和借鉴。比如，境内绿色信贷的纲领性文件《绿色信贷指引》，对环境、安全重大风险企业贷款和节能环保项目及服务贷款进行统计和归纳分类的《绿色信贷统计制度》，以及考核银行开展绿色信贷情况的办法《银行业金融机构绩效考评监管指引》和《绿色信贷实施情况关键评价指标（试行）》等。

其次，部分银行业金融机构制定的绿色信贷内部管理办法和管理流程非常具有借鉴价值。例如工商银行为了实现对客户环境与社会风险的科学量化管理，制定了公司贷款绿色信贷分类标准，以贷款企业或项目对环境影响程度及其面临的环境与社会风险大小，将全部贷款划分为4级、12类，并使分级与客户评级结果相关联。从而为绿色信贷的落地实施奠定了较为坚实的基础。

最后，商业银行在环境信息披露领域能够发挥积极的作用，一方面，商业银行作为重要的资金提供方，在审核和管理贷款企业的同时可以掌握企业的环境表现信息，商业银行完全有可能通过编制、发布指数等方式，向社会披露企业的整体环境表现。另一方面，商业银行也可以通过制定一系列披露规则来引领企业披露环境数据。

（三）银行业为环境风险量化提供工具

尽管全球各国做出了积极的探索，但现实是，环境风险管理工具依然不足，并且已经成为全球银行业发展绿色金融的重要阻碍，导致银行业金融机构在管理环境风险时并不具有明确的针对性，无法对其资产组合面临的环境与社会风险进行量化。面对这样世界性难题的解决方案探索，中国的银行业实际上走在了世界的前头。工商银行率先开展的环境风险对商业银行信用风险的压力测试研究，探索出了环境风险向信用风险的传导机制，测算出了不同程度的环境风险对商业银行信用风险的影响程度，并以部分行业进行了实证测算。这一成果2016年3月在伦敦G20绿色金融会议上发布时，引起了学界和业界的强烈反响，多名专家纷纷赞誉工行的压力测试为全球金融机构开展环境风险量化提供了有效工具。

此外，工商银行近期还开展了"ESG绿色评级与绿色指数"研究，这一研究构建了一套评价企业环境、社会、公司治理表现的指标体系，对上证180公司进行ESG评级，并在此基础上构建指数。我们认为，这一研究是具有一定特色的：一是在指标体系设计和方法上对企业的环境表现赋予较高权重。二是加入工商银行内部大数据，既是对银行独特的数据信息优势的充分挖掘，也是增强指数拟合程度的重要基础。三是基于企业ESG评级分别开发了绿色投资指数和绿色发展指数，在ESG投资产品的设计上进行了有益尝试。四是同时开发了指数运行管理系统和数据来源系统，进一步提升了企业环境数据的质量。

未来，包括工商银行在内的中国银行业将继续深化压力测试研究，在不断拓展覆盖行业和场景的基础上，推广压力测试方法在全球银行业环境与社会风险管理方法上的运用。推动ESG指数的产品化和市场化，运用工商银行大数据帮助市场更好地识别绿色企业，为责任投资者创造价值。

十九大报告为中国绿色金融的发展指明了方向，绘制了蓝图，但我们还应当清醒地认识到，虽然我国的绿色金融已经取得了较多成就，但需要进一步研究、探索、实践的领域还很多。未来，中国银行业将继续与国内外绿色金融业界机构加强合作和沟通，在积极提升自身开展绿色金融能力的同时，继续为建设美丽中国贡献力量，为全世界和谐可持续发展贡献力量。

参考文献：

[1] 张红力，周月秋，马骏，等. 环境因素对商业银行信用风险的影响——基于中国工商银行的压力测试研究与应用[J]. 金融论坛，2016（2）：3-16.

[2] 中国工商银行绿色金融课题组，张红力，周月秋，等. ESG绿色评级及绿色指数研究[J]. 金融论坛，2017（9）：3-14.

[3] 中国工商银行环境因素压力测试课题组,，张红力，周月秋，等. 环境风险压力测试探索[J]. 中国金融，2016（5）：36-38.

[4] 马骏. 中国绿色金融展望[J]. 中国金融，2016（16）：20-22.

[5] 王文，曹明弟. 绿色金融与"一带一路"[J]. 中国金融，2016（16）：25-27.

[6] 周月秋. 绿色金融创新实践的突破[J]. 中国金融，2017（13）：33-34.

[7] 马骏. 发展绿色金融需要大力培育绿色投资者[J]. 当代金融家，2017（1）：17.

[8] 马骏. 地方发展绿色金融大有可为[J]. 中国金融，2017（13）：30-32.

[9] 王遥. 中国绿色金融体系的建构[J]. 建设科技，2017（2）：20.

[10] 殷红. 绿色金融引领"一带一路"绿色化[J]. 中国银行业，2017（4）:60-62.

Outlook on Development Trends of China's Green Finance and Roles of Banking Sector

■ Zhou Yueqiu[1]

Abstract: President Xi Jinping proposes to "accelerate the reform of ecological civilization system" and "develop green finance" in the report of the 19th CPC National Congress. This presents a clear policy signal, indicating that China's green financial system will accelerate its development. The market of green finance will be mature and transparent, a green culture will be recognized and advocated by the whole and China will play a more important role in global governance. China's banking sector will contribute to the development of Chinese and global green finance in multiple fields such as capital support, sharing experiences, tools and methods.

Key words: the 9th CPC National Congress, green finance, global governance and the banking sector

President Xi Jinping pointed out in the report of the 19th CPC National Congress to "accelerate the reform of ecological civilization system and build a beautiful China", and positioned the "development of green finance" as an important way to promote economic green development. This demonstrates China's resolution and faith in improving the environment and realizing sustainable development while consolidating the strategic role of green finance in ecological civilization construction, indicating that China's green finance project will embrace a "golden age" of development and will continue to play a leading role in the world.

[1] By Zhou Yueqiu, Director of ICBC Urban Finance Institute.

Ⅰ. Development Situation of China's Green Finance

Compared with the practices of developed countries, the starting point for China's green finance is not among the earliest ones, but China is among the earliest to uniquely and systematically propose and implement green finance, which has resulted in fast growth and growing influence. Within green finance China has become a world leader in many aspects and has created history.

First, China has the most complete top-level designs within green finance globally. Green finance is highlighted in important framework documents of the Party and the Country such as the report of the 19th CPC National Congress. In August 2016, seven ministries and commissions jointly released the *Guidelines for Establishing the Green Financial System*, which is the first national-level policy document across the world on the development of green finance; in June 2017, China started to build pilot zones for green finance reform and innovation in Zhejiang, Jiangxi, Guangdong, Guizhou and Xinjiang, indicating that China's green finance has entered into the implementation stage of innovation practice.

Second, China's green finance market embraces a rapid development. Green credit size continues to grow, contributing significantly to environmental benefits; the green bond market is witnessing explosive growth, achieving a leap-forward development from nothing to world leader; the national unified carbon finance market is about to start, becoming one of China's important contributions to countering global climate change. The development of green finance products such as green industry development fund, green insurance and green trusts have also begun to accelerate.

Third, China's presidency of the G20 in 2016, China listed green finance as a core topic of the G20 communiqué, which received universal support from G20 countries and directly affected the continued attention to green finance in the 2017 G20 in Germany and 2018 G20 in Argentina.

Ⅱ. Development Trends of China's Green Finance after the 19th CPC National Congress

(i) China will play a more important role in global governance through green finance

China is the world's second largest economy and a major global emitter of greenhouse gases. With strong responsibilities and liabilities, China has made an active contribution to addressing climate change and protecting the earth's environment. In recent years, China has been systematically promoting the system construction, market development and tool innovation of green finance, and comprehensively promoted economically sustainable development and transformation, setting important examples for G20 emerging markets and developing countries. President Xi Jinping pointed out that in the future China will stay committed to building a community of human progress, "sticking to be environmentally friendly", and constructing a "clean and beautiful world", and "protecting the earth on which human lives". Guided by this ambitious goal, green finance will continue to get support from various powers such as governments and the society in China in future, and China's leadership in the field of global green finance will also be strengthened constantly.

China is expected to actively participate in global governance through green finance from two aspects: *On the one hand, by promoting the internationalization of Chinese standards of green finance.* For example, China's green credit index system has been implemented in the banking sector for many years, and surrounding countries have begun to refer to Chinese experience when building their own index systems, so the foundation of global promotion is available. In addition, currently there are not many practices in the field of establishing environmental information disclosure standards, so it is completely possible for China to achieve breakthroughs. *On the other hand, China's has used green finance in leading the construction of "the Belt and Road" project.* Green finance could provide capital, products and information support for the construction of "the Belt and Road", to reduce environmental risks and provide better financing standards. "The Belt and Road" could not be developed without green finance. Meanwhile, by leveraging the global interconnection platform created by "the Belt and Road", China's green finance is also expected to play a more important role in promoting global economic recovery and tackling climate change.

（ⅱ） China's green finance system will become more mature and transparent

Guided by the top-level design, the construction of China's green finance system will become increasingly mature: The green credit market will have stable development, constantly offering green enterprises and projects with convenient and low-cost financing; the green bond market will enter into the stage of steady growth after the end of previous ultra-high-speed growth and, inspired by the lower cost of financing, enterprises and financial institutions are expected to accelerate the pace of issuing green bonds （especially green overseas bonds）; carbon markets will be regulated and unified, and the resulting futures trading will become the highlight of local green finance development; quantitative products and tools such as green indexes will also become more abundant, leading the responsible investment into mainstream.

In addition, the mandatory disclosure mechanism for environmental information of listed companies and bonds issuers is expected to be established, and a more fair, open and transparent market makes the correct pricing of enterprises possible. Meanwhile, under the background of relatively less disclosure practices on environmental information in different countries, China's information disclosure mechanism is expected to become the international standard for such mechanisms.

（ⅲ） Market-driven forces will play a more important role in future

Driven by the policies at the earlier stage and promoted by the supervision and enforcement, the internal impetus of various types of market participants in China are concerned about ecological environment. This has gradually enabled a growing focus on ecological development; at the next stage, "market impetus" will gradually replace "green sensation", playing a more important role in the development of China's green finance.

First, financial institutions have begun to integrate environmental factors into the considerations of capital pricing, which is not only the need of financial institutions to fulfill social responsibility, but also in the strategic choice to prevent environmental and social risks and to find new business growth areas. For example, commercial banks are gradually cutting down and exiting industries with high pollution and high energy consumption, and focusing on enterprises and projects that are environmentally friendly and resource conserving. In the future, enterprises and projects with environmental externalities will have difficulty in getting loans from banks, and at the same time, due to the systematic layout of green finance, have difficulty in getting financial support from other sources. Second, if "difficulty to get financing"and "expensive to get financing"are the reality in the whole finance market, then polluting enterprises will face more severe financing environment and pressure, and will have to be more active to perform business transformation and equipment upgrading, so that the return on investment and profitability of environmental enterprises will increase and the financing cost will decrease gradually. Driven by positive incentives, enterprises will be more actively involved in the market of green finance. Last, promoted by the "pilots in five provinces", the local economy will benefit from the development of green finance. Several provinces are actively deploying and developing green finance, and characterized and personalized development modes, innovative products and services will also appear in succession. The exploration of local green finance markets will provide experience for national green finance development, which is an important supplementation to the "top-down"development mode in China.

(ⅳ) A green culture is recognized and advocated by the whole society

The construction of a beautiful China not only requires the efforts of governments, enterprises and financial institutions, but also requires unified green development values formed in the whole of society. It is stressed in the report of the 19th CPC National Congress that "man and nature are the community of life" , that"modernization with harmonious coexistence of man and nature should be constructed", and that the environment for common participation and common governance by all people should be advocated. After the 19th CPC National Congress, green development is becoming more popular as an important directory for people to pay attention to and work hard towards. In capital markets, the ESG (environmental, social and corporate governance) investment has been recognized by more and more investors; in addition to financial performance, corporate environmental performance and social image have become important factors of corporate pricing for investors to consider. Meanwhile, we are also delighted to see that green finance has already appeared in campuses and classrooms. Central University of Finance and Economics and Renmin University of China have set up master's major and course of green finance, which will generate positive impacts on shaping a new generation of green finance values in China and training more professional talents on green finance.

Ⅲ. China's banking sector is the mainstay for promoting green finance development

(ⅰ) Banking sector provides capital support for green financing

As the largest capital provider in China's financial market, the banking sector has for a long time provided massive capital support for supporting the construction of a substantial economy and promoted the

sustainable transformation of the economic structure. Certainly, the banking sector is also the largest capital provider in green financing markets. As of the end of February 2017, the green credit balance of 21 major banking institutions in China reached RMB 7.5 trillion accounting for 9.0% of all loans. It is expected to save 193 million tons of standard coal, reduce the emission of 449 million tons of carbon dioxide, 4.1 million tons of chemical oxygen demand, 449million tons of ammonia nitrogen, 4.1 million tons of sulfur dioxide and 2.0722 million tons of nitric oxide, and save 644 million tons of water.

With constant deepening and promotion of the strategy of ecological civilization, the capital amount required for the development of green industry is increasing. The banking sector should actively innovate financing modes, expand financing channels, and improve financing capacity, so as to constantly contribute to the green development of China's economy. In the past two years, China's green bond markets have embraced rapid development, and received intensive concerns by international investors; commercial banks in China have also actively started the issuance of overseas green bonds, building a bridge for overseas capital to support the construction of China's green industries: All major banks are active in this field. Particularly, ICBC issued the first "Belt and Road" green climate bonds in Luxembourg on November 28, 2017, raising capital of USD 2.15 billion, for the two 3-year products issued in Euro and US dollar. European investors accounted for over 70% of subscription. The capital raised through this green bond will be used to support four types of qualified green credit projects already launched or to be launched by ICBC, i.e., renewable energy, low-carbon and low-emission transportation, energy efficiency,

and sustainable water management.

The interest rate spread of the green bond issued was also at the best level comparable with Chinese capital, and broke several records at the time, e.g., the first bond simultaneously meeting international and Chinese domestic new green bond standards; the first green bond of Chinese-funded institutions receiving the second opinions of the Center for International Climate and Environmental Research in Oslo （CICERO） and the unique highest praise of "dark green" so far. The first bond of Chinese-funded financial institutions certified by bond certified by Climate Bonds Initiative （CBI）; the first green bond within green projects along"the Belt and Road", as well as being the Chinese-funded green bond with largest single issuance amount in Euro.

（ⅱ） The banking sector provides existing experience for the development of green finance

First, the financial institutions in the banking sector in China have accumulated extensive practical experience after years of operation and management. The policies and systems related to green credit can also provide reference for China to improve the green finance system. For example, the *Green Credit Guidelines* which is a Chinese framework document on green credit, the *Statistics System on Green Credit* performing statistical and inductive classification on the loans of enterprises with major environmental and security risks and the loans for energy conservation and environmental protection projects and service, the *Guideline on Assessing and Monitoring the Performance of Financial Institutions in Banking Sector,* and the *Key Assessment Indicators on the Implementation of Green Credit （Trial）* assessing the business of green credit in banks.

Second, the internal management methods and management procedures for green credit developed by some financial institutions in the banking sector are of great reference value. For example, in order to realize a scientifically quantitative management of environment and social risks, ICBC has developed the classification standards for corporate green credit, classifying all loans into 4 grades within 12 categories according to the influence of loan enterprises or projects on the environment and the social risks of such projects, and linking such grading with client assessment results. This lays a relatively solid foundation for the implementation of green credit.

Last, commercial banks can play a positive role in the field of environmental information disclosure. On the one hand, as important providers of capital, commercial banks may obtain the information on enterprises' environmental performance when reviewing and management the loan enterprises, and it is possible for commercial banks to disclose the general environmental performance of enterprises to the public by compiling and releasing indexes. On the other hand, commercial banks can guide enterprises to disclose environmental data by developing a series of disclosure rules.

（iii） The banking sector provides tools for the quantification of environmental risks

Although many countries in the world have made positive efforts, the reality is that environmental risk management tools are still insufficient, and this has become an important obstacle for the development of the global banking sector. This results in financial institutions without specific targets for managing environmental risks and failure to quantify the environmental and social risks of their investment portfolio. When seeking solutions for such worldwide problems, China's banking sector has become a world leader. The stress test and study on the environmental risks and the credit risks of commercial banks first carried out by ICBC has explored a mechanism for the transmission from environmental risks to credit risks, measured the impacts of different degrees of environmental risks on the credit risks of commercial banks, and performed empirical estimates in some industries. This result, when released at the London G20 Green Finance Conference in March 2016, caused intensive responses from the academics and the industry in that many experts praised that the stress test by ICBC had provided effective tools for global financial institutions to carry out the quantification of environmental risks.

In addition, ICBC recently launched the "ESG green rating and green index" research, which established a set of index systems for assessing the environmental, social and corporate governance performance of enterprises, performing ESG rating for 180 enterprises listed on the Shanghai Stock Exchange, and developed indexes on this basis. We hold that this research has certain characteristics: First, higher weight is given to the environmental performance of enterprises in the design of index system and methods. Second, the internal big data of ICBC is included, which is not only a sufficient excavation of the unique data information superiority of the bank, but also an important foundation for enhancing the degree of index fitting. Third, green investment indexes and

green development indexes are developed respectively based on corporate ESG rating, and beneficial attempts are made in the design of ESG investment products; fourth, index operation management system and data source system are developed simultaneously to further improve the quality of corporate environmental data.

In the future, China's banking sector, including ICBC, will continue to deepen the stress test study, and on the basis of expanding the covered industries and cases, promote the application of stress test methods within the environmental and social risk management of the global banking sector. It will also promote the commercialization and marketization of ESG indexes and ICBC big data to help markets better identify green enterprises and create value for responsible investors.

The report of the 19th CPC National Congress pointed out the direction and drew the blueprint for the development of China's green finance, but we should be clear that though China has made tremendous achievements in the field of green finance, there are still many fields requiring further study, exploration and practice. In the future, China's banking sector will continue to strengthen cooperation and communication with domestic and foreign green financial institutions. While being active in improving the capacity in green finance, the sector will continue to make contributions to building a beautiful China and to achieving a harmonious and sustainable development in the world.

References:

[1] ICBC Green Finance Research Group, Zhang Hongli, Zhou Yueqiu et al. Study on ESG Green Rating and Green Indicators [J]. Finance Forum, 2017（9）:3-14.

[2] ICBC Environmental Factors Stress Test Group, Zhang Hongli, Zhou Yueqiu et al. Study on Environmental Risks Stress Test [J]. China Finance, 2016（5）:36-38.

[3] Ma Jun. Outlook on China's Green Finance [J]. China Finance, 2016（16）:20-22.

[4] Ma Jun. The Development of Green Finance Requires Vigorous Development of Green Investors [J]. Modern Bankers, 2017（1）:17.

[5] Ma Jun. Great Potential for Developing Local Green Finance [J]. China Finance, 2017（13）:30-32.

[6] Wang Yao. Construction of China's Green Finance System [J]. Construction Science and Technology, 2017（2）:20.

[7] Wang Wen, Cao Mingdi. Green Finance and "the Belt and Road" [J]. China Finance, 2016（16）:25-27.

[8] Yin Hong. Green Finance Leading the Greenization of "the Belt and Road" . China Banking Association, 2017（4）:60-62.

[9] Zhang Hongli, Zhou Yueqiu, Ma Jun et al. Impacts of Environmental Factors on Credit Risks of Commercial Banks - Study and Application Based on the Stress Test of ICBC [J]. Finance Forum, 2016（2）:3-16.

[10] Zhou Yueqiu. Breakthrough of Green Finance Innovation Practice [J]. China Finance, 2017（13）:33-34.

中国绿色资产证券化的现状分析及发展建议

■ 周亚成[1]

摘要：本文首先定义了何为绿色资产证券化，分析了绿色资产证券化的融资优势，并通过对绿色资产证券化现有政策环境和已发行产品的梳理，从给予税收优惠、丰富资产类型、鼓励绿色资产证券化与PPP相结合等方面提出了促进我国绿色资产证券化发展的建议。

关键词：绿色金融　绿色资产证券化　现状分析　发展建议

习近平总书记在中国共产党第十九次全国代表大会上的报告中指出，要"发展绿色金融，壮大节能环保产业、清洁生产产业、清洁能源产业"。节能环保产业、清洁生产产业、清洁能源产业的壮大必须依靠绿色金融的资金支持，绿色金融的发展则需要各种绿色金融产品的创新和运用。绿色资产证券化具有独特的融资优势，是发展绿色金融不可或缺的组成部分。

一、绿色资产证券化的定义

就绿色公司债券，证监会在《关于支持绿色债券发展的指导意见》中将其定义为：符合《证券法》《公司法》《公司债券发行与交易管理办法》及其他相关法律法规的规定，遵循证券交易所相关业务规则的要求，募集资金用于支持绿色产业项目的公司债券。

参照前述定义，结合资产证券化的特殊性，本文将绿色资产支持证券定义为：依照相关法律法规发行的、募集资金专项用于支持绿色项目的资产支持证券。绿色资产证券化就是绿色资产支持证券的动态发行过程。与绿色企业债券、绿色金融债券、绿色公司债券等绿色融资工具相同的是，绿色资产支持证券的募集资金也须专项用于

---

[1] 周亚成，北京市中伦律师事务所合伙人，中国金融学会绿色金融专业委员会副秘书长、理事及金融法规小组牵头人。

支持绿色项目；但与绿色债券不同的是，为绿色资产支持证券提供偿付支持的基础资产本身也可能属于绿色项目（如污水处理厂的服务费、水电站的上网电费等），以该现金流为偿付支持的资产支持证券即属于"双绿"项目，具有更好的环境效益。

二、绿色资产证券化的融资优势

作为一种融资工具，资产支持证券自2014年以来在我国发展迅猛，受到融资方、资管机构、投资人的追捧，资产规模已突破3万亿元。借助资产支持证券的以下融资优势，将资产支持证券引入绿色证券市场，对于发展绿色金融、推动绿色发展具有重要的积极意义。

（一）拓宽融资渠道

通过灵活的交易结构设置、结构化安排，资产支持证券在资本市场的接受度更高，可为绿色项目增加一条融资渠道。

（二）降低融资门槛

资产支持证券以基础资产所产生的现金流作为偿付支持，并通过"真实出售"将基础资产与融资主体进行破产隔离，因此，与传统融资工具注重融资主体的主体信用不同，资产支持证券更加注重基础资产的信用评价。对于那些主体信用不高但拥有良好绿色项目的融资者，更易于通过发行资产支持证券获得融资。

（三）实现会计出表

现行监管规则对融资租赁企业、商业银行等金融机构均存在一定的资本杠杆率要求。例如，银监会《商业银行资本管理办法》第二十三条规定："商业银行各级资本充足率不得低于如下最低要求：（三）资本充足率不得低于8%。"商务部《融资租赁企业监督管理办法》第二十二条规定："融资租赁企业的风险资产不得超过净资产总额的10倍。"而实际的资本充足率受到监管机构的严格指导，比法律规定的比例更高，以四大国有商业银行为例，其资本充足率普遍在18%左右。因此，商业银行、融资租赁企业往往具有通过真实出售实现会计出表的需求。绿色资产证券化通过出售作为基础资产的风险资产，可以实现会计出表。也就是说，商业银行可以将其应收贷款、融资租赁企业可以将其应收租赁款作为基础资产，发行绿色资产支持证券，实现相关风险资产的会计出表，优化财务结构。

三、绿色资产证券化的政策环境

自中共中央、国务院于2015年9月印发《生态文明体制改革总体方案》，提出"建立绿色金融体系"后，中国人民银行、财政部、发展改革委、环境保护部、银监会、证监会、保监会七部门于2016年8月31日联合发布了《关于构建绿色金融体系的指导意见》，对构建绿色金融体系提出了八项具体的指导意见。在这两份纲领性政策文件的基础上，相关监管部门、行业自律组织先后出台了各种通知、指引等规范性文件指导绿色债券的发行。目前已发布的规范性文件主要包括：

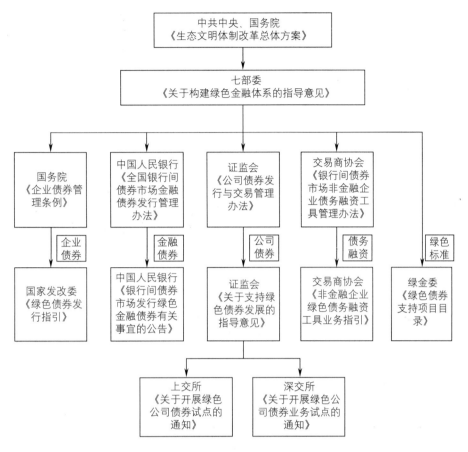

图1　绿色债券政策法规体系

由图1可知，目前，各监管机构对于企业债券、金融债券、债务融资工具、公司债券等债券品种均出台了相应的政策法规，指导绿色债券的发行。同时，中国金融学会绿色金融专业委员会编制了我国第一份关于绿色债券界定与分类的文件——《绿色债券支持项目目录》，为绿色债券审批与注册、第三方绿色债券评估、绿色债券评级和相关信息披露提供参考依据。前述规则原则上鼓励绿色资产证券化的发展，并规定绿色资产证券化的发行可参照前述规则执行。

总体来说，我国对各主要债券品种均已出台相应规则以指导绿色债券的发行。但是，这些规则不够全面、具体，缺乏指导性，尚需监管层和市场参与主体不断补充、完善。至于绿色资产证券化，目前尚无具体的、专门的规则指引。

四、已发行产品及其特点

截至2017年11月，据笔者不完全统计，市场已发行绿色资产支持证券15单，募集资金240.46亿元（详情请见表1 已发行绿色资产支持证券产品信息汇总表）。分析表1的各项信息和数据，目前市场上已发行的绿色资产支持证券呈现出以下特点：

（一）绿色企业资产证券化位居首位

区分监管部门的不同，我国目前的资产证券化主要分为中国人民银行、银监会主管的信贷资产证券化、证监会主管的企业资产证券化、中国银行间市场交易商协会主管的资产支持票据以及保监会主管的项目资产支持计划。从表1来看，已发行绿色资产支持证券主要集中

于绿色企业资产支持证券，绿色信贷资产支持证券只有两单。绿色信贷资产证券化的市场冷淡与我国绿色信贷本身发展滞后存在着一定的关联。已发行的两单绿色信贷资产支持证券均由兴业银行发行，这与兴业银行长期耕耘于绿色信贷业务密不可分。

（二）基础资产类型单一

就基础资产而言，已发行产品主要集中在污水处理收费收益权、公交经营收费收益权、电力上网收费收益权以及绿色贷款方面。《绿色债券支持项目目录》包含的31类项目中还有大量可据以发行资产支持证券的基础资产有待市场开发和运用。

（三）信用级别普遍较高

在已发行的绿色资产证券化产品中，评级机构普遍给予了基础资产AAA级别的信用评级。这样的高评级现象完全符合绿色资产证券化的内在特点：即绿色项目对环境友好，符合国家的产业政策，更易获得较高的信用评级。

（四）融资成本总体较高

表1显示，2017年以来，绿色资产支持证券的平均发行利率在5%以上。金融界发布的《联合信用：2017年10月利差分析报告》显示，2017年10月，AAA级普通资产支持证券的平均发行利率为5.33%[1]。与普通资产支持证券相比，绿色资产支持证券的融资成本较高，并未突显其融资优势。这可能与绿色资产证券化刚刚推出、市场尚在观望中以及政府的政策扶持未到位等因素有关。

（五）发行人注重绿色评估

15单已发行的产品中，至少7单委托独立的评估机构对基础资产以及募集资金投向进行了评估，这7单证券均取得了交易所的绿色贴标（即

在证券简称前标注G，以示区别）。

（六）资金流向绿色项目

虽无法掌握所有已发行产品募集资金的具体用途，但根据绿色资产支持证券的应有之义，绿色资产支持证券所募集的资金应严格投向绿色项目。由于绿色资产支持证券所募集资金应严格用于绿色项目，如募集资金用于偿还银行借款，该借款亦应是为绿色项目提供。

五、绿色资产证券化的发展建议

虽然市场上已相继出现各类绿色资产支持证券，但相较于成熟的债券市场以及发展较快的绿色债券，我国的绿色资产证券化尚处于起步阶段。一方面，我国的绿色产业发展具有巨大的资金需求，另一方面，绿色资产证券化因其特有的融资优势，能够较好地为绿色产业提供融资通道。因此，可以展望的是，我国的绿色资产证券化大有可为，具有广阔的发展空间。但是，期待绿色资产证券化快速发展的同时，我们也应当从已进行的绿色资产支持证券发行实践中总结经验，以保障我国的绿色资产证券化健康、有序地发展。为此，笔者提出以下建议：

（一）加强政策扶持，给予税收优惠

绿色资产证券化会发生基础资产的转移，其不仅是一项融资行为，也是一项买卖行为，涉及的税务问题比其他绿色金融产品复杂，其对政策扶持（特别是税收优惠政策）的需求也更加强烈。

现阶段，绿色资产证券化在资产转移、取得项目收益、证券二级市场流转等主要环节均存在一定的税负问题（主要从所得税和增值税两方面进行分析）。就资产转移环节而言，融资方将

---

[1] 网址http://bond.jrj.com.cn/2017/12/05163423743850.shtml，最后一次访问于2017年12月12日。

基础资产转移给特殊目的实体时，融资方取得了《企业所得税法》规定的所得，需要缴纳企业所得税。对于转让应收款项类债权资产，现行税收体系并未明确债权转让是否征收增值税以及按照何种项目征收。就取得项目收益环节而言，融资方（此时的角色是资产服务机构）因基础资产取得收入时，会产生增值税，该等收入自资产服务机构支付至特殊目的实体以及自特殊目的实体分配给投资者时，都可能分别产生增值税。就证券二级市场流转环节而言，投资者之间买卖绿色资产支持证券需缴纳所得税，并按照《营业税改征增值税试点实施办法》规定的"金融商品转让"项目缴纳增值税。

绿色资产证券化需要税收优惠政策的扶持，税收优惠政策是国家利用税收调节经济的具体手段，对扶持特殊产业的发展具有重要作用。七部委《关于构建绿色金融体系的指导意见》即提出，建立健全绿色金融体系，需要金融、财政、环保等政策和相关法律法规的配套支持。为此，笔者建议，绿色资产证券化监管部门与税务部门一同研究制定相关规定，明确绿色资产证券化交易中的税收处理规则以及支持绿色资产证券化交易的税收优惠政策，以降低交易成本，充分调动发行人、资管机构以及投资人对发行、购买绿色资产支持证券的积极性。唯有市场参与者的积极参与，才能极大地激活绿色资产证券化市场的潜力，促进绿色金融和绿色产业的发展。

（二）鼓励双绿项目，丰富资产类型

绿色资产支持证券的基础资产虽不限于绿色项目，但应当鼓励以绿色基础资产发行绿色资产支持证券，实现来源和用途的"双绿"。从已发行的资产支持证券产品来看，基础资产虽多属于绿色项目，但主要集中在污水处理收费收益

权、公交经营收费收益权、电力上网收费收益权以及绿色贷款方面，而绿色项目的类型远远不止于此。气候债券倡议组织（The Climate Bonds Initiative）制定的《气候债券标准》（CBS）包含了8大类44小类绿色项目，而作为中国版绿色标准的《绿色债券支持项目目录》也包含了6大类31小类绿色项目。此外，就绿色信贷来看，据银监会公布的数据，截至2016年6月末，21家主要银行业金融机构绿色信贷余额达7.26万亿元，占各项贷款的9.0%[1]。由此可见，绿色信贷资产证券化的资产体量巨大，而实际发行的规模却极小。理论上讲，只要绿色项目能够产生稳定的现金流，且项目业主保证将募集资金用于绿色项目，就能发行绿色资产支持证券。因此，建议监管层鼓励市场创新，丰富证券化的基础资产类型，激活市场潜力。

（三）鼓励绿色资产证券化与PPP相结合

政府和社会资本合作模式（PPP）的通常模式是由社会资本承担设计、建设、运营、维护基础设施的大部分工作，并通过"使用者付费"及必要的"政府付费"获得合理投资回报。PPP是国家确定的重大经济改革任务，对于加快新型城镇化建设、提升国家治理能力、构建现代财政制度具有重要意义。

目前已经公布的PPP项目中，有相当部分涉及绿色产业，包括新能源汽车公共充电设施、污水处理厂、污泥餐厨（垃圾）处置、垃圾处理设施、生态综合整治、园林绿化等。根据财政部PPP中心公布的《第三批示范项目分析报告》，生态建设和环境保护类项目共计46个，投资总额810.56亿元，项目数量占比8.9%，投资总额占比6.9%。

---

[1] 中国经济网，银监会：绿色信贷助推经济结构调整，http://finance.ce.cn/rolling/201609/03/t20160903_15551168.shtml，最后一次访问于2017年12月1日。

然而，由于绿色产业存在回报周期长、投资者退出渠道不畅等相关问题，社会资本投资PPP项目的积极性普遍不高。将绿色资产证券化与PPP相结合则能较好地解决这一问题：首先，通过资产证券化，发起人可一次性取得项目未来的现金流，满足PPP项目投资者即时退出的要求（当然，根据绿色资产证券化的核心内涵，PPP项目投资者应承诺将募集资金再投向其他绿色项目）；其次，资产证券化结构灵活，可发行存续期较长的产品，适应PPP回款期较长的特点；再次，PPP项目具有稳定的现金流，天然适宜证券化。因此，对于绿色PPP项目，可以通过资产证券化方式，将未来的现金流提前变现，加快投资人的资金回收周期，便于吸引更多社会资本参与绿色产业。[1]而对于绿色资产证券化，主动介入绿色PPP项目，既可以为绿色PPP项目提供资金支持，也可以扩大绿色资产证券化的规模，增强市场对绿色资产证券化的认识。因此，绿色资产证券化与PPP双管齐下，可有效促进绿色产业的发展。

（四）鼓励信息披露，设立评价规则

目前，上市公司越来越重视企业的社会责任，笔者认为，参与绿色金融也应当属于企业社会责任的一部分。为此，笔者建议建立相应的披露规则，要求上市公司（主要包括环境污染企业以及从事绿色产业的企业）、资产管理人、机构投资者等绿色金融的主要参与者披露其参与绿色金融的情况，包括参与绿色金融的基本情况、发行或投资绿色金融产品占本披露主体已发行或投资金融产品的比例等，如未参与绿色金融，亦应明确披露未参与。同时，应设立相应的评价规则，对于重视该等披露的主体，可考虑设置奖

励、简化其相关审核工作等激励措施。

绿色金融是将金融引入绿色项目的重大举措，既能促进产业升级发展，又符合环境公共利益。资产证券化作为一种灵活、精准的投融资工具，其与绿色产业的结合将进一步满足绿色产业的资金需求，推动绿色产业的快速发展。在十九大报告提纲挈领的宏伟蓝图下，中国的绿色金融必将焕发更加蓬勃的生机。

参考文献：

[1] 马骏.中国绿色金融发展的十个领域[J].武汉金融，2017（1）.

[2] 马骏.中国绿色金融的发展与前景[J].经济社会体制比较，2016（6）.

[3] 洪艳蓉.绿色债券运作机制的国际规则与启示[J].法学，2017（2）.

[4] 朱晋，李永坤.绿色产业资产证券化融资方式及金融机构介入模式探析[J].现代管理科学，2017（10）.

[5] 中国人民银行杭州中心支行办公室课题组.绿色金融：国际经验、启示及对策[J].货币银行，2011（5）.

[6] 环境保护部环境规划院.中国绿色金融政策年度报告2016[J].财之道，2017（8）.

[7] 曹萍.绿色资产证券化创新发展大有可为[EB].证券时报网，2016年3月22日。

[8] 绿色资产证券化探析[EB].中国金融信息网，2016年9月2日。

---

[1] 新华网，绿色资产证券化兴起 助力供给侧改革，http://news.xinhuanet.com/finance/2016-03/03/c_128769279.htm，最后访问于2017年12月1日。

表1 已发行绿色资产支持证券产品信息汇总表[1]

序号	产品名称	设立日	发行主体	基础资产	发行规模（亿元）	信用评级	平均发行利率	是否进行绿色评估（认证机构）	是否贴标	资金用途
1	嘉实资本中节能绿色建筑资产支持专项计划	2017/11/02	中国节能环保集团公司	成都国际科技节能大厦	8.20	AAA	5.20%	/	否	/
2	南通市经济技术开发区污水处理收费收益权资产支持专项计划	2017/09/15	南通市经济技术开发区公司	污水处理收费收益权	5.10	AA+	6.30%	是（北京中财绿融咨询有限公司）	是	河道疏浚等整体环境提升项目
3	特锐德应收账款一期绿色资产支持专项计划	2017/09/14	青岛特锐德电气股份有限公司	应收账款债权	9.83	AAA AA A+	6.30%	/	否	新能源汽车充电设施项目的建设运营
4	桑德北京水务一期绿色资产支持专项计划	2017/08/23	北京京禹顺环保有限公司	污水处理服务费收益权	8.20	AA+	6.50%	是（北京商道融绿咨询有限公司）	是	偿还融资租赁债务，顺义区污水处理厂二期扩建项目和三期改扩建建设
5	葛洲坝绿园绿色应收账款一期资产支持专项计划	2017/08/10	葛洲坝环嘉（大连）再生资源有限公司 葛洲坝兴业再生资源有限公司	应收账款债权	13.04	AA+ AA	6.50%	/	是	/
6	中国中投证券—武汉地铁信托受益权一期绿色资产支持专项计划	2017/07/18	武汉市轨道交通建设有限公司	信托受益权	15.00	AAA	5.07%	/	是	/
7	平安—贵阳公交经营收费收益权绿色资产支持专项计划	2017/03/29	贵阳市公共交通(集团)有限公司	公交经营收费收益权	26.50	AAA	5.72%	是（北京中财绿融咨询有限公司）	是	贵阳公交绿色产业项目的建设和运营

[1] 数据根据互联网公布的信息整理、汇总。

续表

序号	产品名称	设立日	发行主体	基础资产	发行规模（亿元）	信用评级	平均发行利率	是否进行绿色评估（认证机构）	是否贴标	资金用途
8	华泰资管—葛洲坝水电上网收费权绿色资产支持专项计划	2016/11/22	中国葛洲坝集团股份有限公司	水电上网收费收益权	8.00	AAA	3.41%	是（北京中财绿融咨询有限公司）	是	水电站的再融资
9	无锡交通产业集团公交收费收益权绿色资产支持专项计划	2016/09/28	无锡市交通产业集团有限公司	公交经营收费收益权	19.80	AAA	3.72%	是	是	公交车辆的购置（以新能源公交车和清洁能源公交车为主）、公交设施运营
10	农银穗盈—金风科技风电收费收益权专项计划	2016/08/03	新疆金风科技股份有限公司	风电收费收益权	12.75	AAA	3.92%	是（挪威船级社.DC）	是	偿还公司的待偿还银行借款以及补充公司或项目公司的流动资金
11	募实节能1号资产支持专项计划	2015/10/16	中国节能环保集团有限公司	生活垃圾焚烧发电电力收费收益权	6.80	AAA	/	/	否	/
12	兴银2016年第一期绿色金融信贷资产支持证券	2016/01/07	兴业银行股份有限公司	绿色贷款	26.46	AAA. A+	3.56%	/	否	/
13	兴元2014年第二期绿色金融信贷资产支持证券	2014/09/18	兴业银行股份有限公司	绿色贷款	34.94	AAA A+ /AA	5.50%	/	否	/
14	中电投融和融资租赁有限公司2017年度第一期绿色资产支持票据	2017/06/29	中电投融和融资租赁有限公司	租赁债权和其他权利及其附属担保权	24.84	AAA AA	/	是（中诚信国际信用评级有限责任公司）	否	/
15	北控水务（中国）投资有限公司2017年第一期绿色资产支持票据	2017/04/25	北控水务（中国）投资有限公司	污水处理费收益权	21.00	AAA	5.03%	是（北京商道融绿咨询有限公司）	否	绿色项目建设、补充公司流动资金

Analysis of Current Situation and Development Suggestions on China's Green Asset Securitization

■ Zhou Yacheng[1]

Abstract: This paper provides definitions within green asset securitization, analyzes the financing advantages of green asset securitization, and proposes suggestions on promoting the development of China's green asset securitization. This is done by sorting out the existing policy environments within green asset securitization with regards to tax preference, an expansion of asset types, and the encouragement of green asset securitization within a Public-Private-Partnership（PPP）framework.

Key words: Green finance, green asset securitization, current situation analysis, and development suggestions

President Xi Jinping pointed out in the report of the 19th CPC National Congress to "develop green finance, and expand energy conservation and environmental protection industries, clean production industry, and clean energy industry". The expansion of such industries must rely on the capital support from green finance, while the development of green finance requires the innovation and application of various types of green finance products. With unique financing advantages, green asset securitization is an indispensable part of green finance.

I . Definition of green asset securitization

Green corporate bonds are defined as follows in the *Guiding Opinions on Supporting the Development of Green Bonds* by China Securities Regulatory Commission: The corporate bond that raises capital for green industry projects must be in accordance with

---

[1] Zhou Yacheng, partner of Beijing Zhong Lun Law Firm; Deputy Secretary General of Green Finance Committee, China Society for Finance & Banking, and initiator of Financial Regulations Group.

the *Securities Law*, the *Company Law*, the *Administrative Measures for the Issuance and Trading of Corporate Bonds* and other applicable laws and regulations, and in line with relevant business rules of stock exchanges.

According to the above definition and taking into consideration the particularities of asset securitization, this paper defines green asset-backed securities as follows: Asset-backed securities that are issued according to relevant laws and regulations and raises special capital to support green projects. Green asset securitization is a dynamic issuance process of green asset-backed securities. Same with green financing instruments such as green enterprise bonds, green finance bonds and green corporate bonds, the raised capital through green asset-backed securities shall be used specifically to support green projects; however, different from green bonds, basic assets provide reimbursement support for green asset-backed securities belonging to green projects themselves（e.g., service charge of sewage treatment works, grid electricity charge of hydropower stations, etc.）, and the asset-backed securities at the end of this cash flow are reimbursed support and belongs to "dual-green" projects and thus have better environmental benefits.

Ⅱ. Financing advantages of green asset securitization

As a financing instrument, asset-backed securities have embraced a rapid development in China since 2014 and a high popularity among financiers, capital management institutions and investors, with the accumulated asset class already exceeding RMB 3 trillion. Leveraging the following financing advantages of asset-backed securities to introduce asset-backed securities into green securities market is of great and active significance for developing green finance and promoting green development.

（ⅰ）Broaden financing channels

Through flexible setting of trading structures and structural arrangements, asset-backed securities are more acceptable to capital markets, which adds a financing channel for green projects.

（ⅱ）Reduce financing threshold

Asset-backed securities take the cash flow generated by basic assets as reimbursement support, and perform bankruptcy isolation between basic assets and financing participants through "real sales"; therefore, unlike traditional financing instruments focusing on the credit of financing participants, asset-backed securities focus more on credit assessment of basic assets. Financiers without high participant credit, but with good green projects, may obtain financing easier through the issuance of asset-backed securities.

（ⅲ）Accounting statements

Existing regulations have certain capital leverage requirements on financial institutions such as finance leasing enterprises and commercial banks. For example, Article 23 of the *Administrative Measures for the Capital of Commercial Banks*（Trial）stipulates that "The capital adequacy ratio of commercial banks at different levels shall not be lower than the following minimum requirements:（Ⅲ）Capital adequacy ratio shall not be less than 8%." Article 22 of the Administrative Measures for the Supervision on Financial Leasing Enterprises issued by the Ministry of Commerce stipulates that "risky assets of financial leasing enterprises shall not exceed 10 times that of the total net assets."The actual capital adequacy ratio is strictly monitored by the regulator and is higher than what is stipulated in law. Take the four state-owned commercial banks as examples, the capital adequacy ratio is generally about 14%. Therefore, commercial banks and financial leasing enterprises often have to answer to demands of realizing accounting statements through real sales. Green asset securitization may realize accounting statements by selling the risky assets which are basic ones. That is, commercial banks can take their loan receivables, and financial leasing enterprises can take their lease payment receivables, as basic assets, issue green asset-backed securities, realize accounting statements of relevant risky assets, and optimize the financial structure.

III. Policy environment of green asset securitization

After the CPC Central Committee and the State Council issued the *Integrated Reform Plan for Promoting Ecological Progress,* proposing to "construct a green finance system" in September 2015, seven ministries and commissions （People's Bank of China, Ministry of Finance, State Development and Reform Commission, Ministry of Environmental Protection, China Banking Regulatory Commission, China Securities Regulatory Commission and China Insurance Regulatory Commission） jointly released the *Guidelines to Construct the Green Financial System* on August 31, 2016, proposing eight specific guiding opinions on the construction of a green finance system. Based on the two guiding policy documents, relevant regulators and industrial self-regulatory organizations successively issued various normative documents to guide the issuance of green bonds. The normative documents currently issued include:

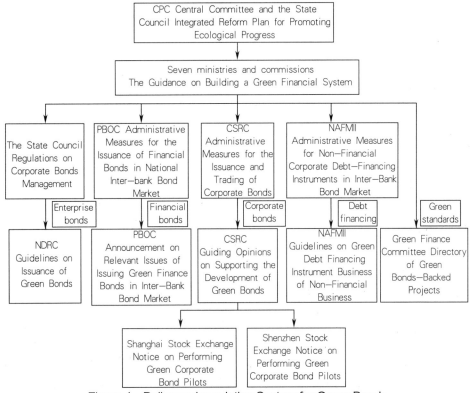

Figure 1   Policy and regulation System for Green Bonds

According to Figure 1, various regulator institutions have currently released corresponding policies and regulations for different types of bonds such as enterprise bonds, financial bonds, debt financing instruments and corporate bonds, so as to guide the issuance of green bonds. Meanwhile, Green Finance Committee under China Society for Finance & Banking have compiled the first document on the definition and classification of green finance in China, *Directory of Green Bonds-Backed Projects,* offering reference basis for the approval and registration of green bonds, the third-party assessment of green bonds, the grading of green bonds, and the disclosure of relevant information. In principle, the above regulations encourage the development of green asset securitization, and stipulate that the issuance of green asset securitization may refer to the above regulations for implementation.

Generally, China has released corresponding regulations for major types of bonds to guide the issuance of green bonds. However, such regulations are not comprehensive and lack guidance, so constant supplementations by regulators and market participants are required. For green asset securitization, currently there are no specific and special regulations for guidance.

IV. Issued products and their characteristics

The incomplete statistics indicates that as of November 2017, 15 green asset-backed securities had been issued in the market, raising a total capital of RMB 24.046 billion (see details in Table 1 Summarization of Green Asset-Backed Securities Products Already Issued) . According to the analysis of the information and data in Table 1, the green asset-backed securities already issued in the market have the following characteristics:

(i) Green enterprise asset securitization tops the list

China's current asset securitization is mainly classified into the credit asset securitization under PBOC and CBRC, enterprise asset securitization under CSRC, asset-backed notes under China's National Association of Financial Market Institutional Investors (NAFMII) , and the project asset-backed plans under CIRC. According to Table 1, the green asset-backed securities already issued are mainly green enterprise asset-backed securities, and there are so far only two green credit asset-backed securities. The size of the market for green credit asset securitization is partly due to the lagging development of China's green credit sector. The two green credit asset-backed securities were issued by Industrial Bank, which is the result of the long-term commitment of Industrial Bank in green credit business.

(ii) Basic assets have single types

For basic assets, the issued products are mainly concentrated in the right to earnings from sewage disposal charges, the right to earnings from public transport operation charges, the right to earnings from grid electricity charges and the green loans. In the 31 categories of projects included in the *Directory of Green Bonds-Backed Projects,* there are many basic assets available for market development and application of asset-backed securities.

(iii) Credit levels are generally higher

The green asset securitization products

already issued are rated by the rating agencies universally has received a Credit Grade AAA for basic assets. The high rating fully meets the internal characteristics of green asset securitization, i.e., green projects are friendly to the environment and meet national industrial policies, thus being making it easier for them to obtain higher credit rating.

(iv) Financing costs are generally higher

According to Table 1, the average issuing interest rate of green asset-backed securities has been above 5% since 2017. The *Joint Credit: October 2017 Spreads Analysis Report* issued by JRJ.COM indicates that the average issuing interest rate of Grade AAA ordinary asset-backed securities was 5.33% in October 2017.[1] Compared with ordinary asset-backed securities, the financing cost of green asset-backed securities is relatively high and has no highlighted financing advantage. The reasons may be that green asset securitization was just launched recently, hence the markets are still on the sidelines, and the supporting policies are not in place.

(v) Issuers highlight green assessment

Among the 15 issued products at least 7 were entrusted to independent assessment agencies for the assessment of the investment of basic assets and raised capital, and these 7 products obtained the green label from stock exchanges.

(vi) Capital flows to green projects

Though the specific purposes of the capital raised by all issued products is difficult to obtain, the proper connotation of green asset-backed securities requires that the capital raised by green asset-backed securities should be invested strictly in green projects. Since the capital raised by green asset-backed securities should be invested strictly in green projects, hence, if the raised capital is used for the repayment of bank loans, such loans should also be used for green projects.

V. Development Suggestions on Green Asset Securitization

Though various types of asset-backed securities appear successively in markets, compared with the relatively mature bond market and the fast-growing green bonds, China's green asset securitization is still at the initial stage. On one hand, China's green industry has huge capital demands. On the other hand, due to the unique financing advantages, green asset securitization may better provide financing channels for green industry. Therefore, it can be expected that China's green asset securitization industry will have great potential and a broad development space. However, when expecting the rapid development of green asset securitization, we also ought to sum up the experience from the issuance practice of green asset-backed securities, so as to ensure the healthy and orderly development of green asset securitization in China. Therefore, the author proposes the following suggestions:

---

[1] Website: http://bond.jrj.com.cn/2017/12/05163423743850.shtml, last accessed on December 12, 2017.

（i） Strengthen policy support and provide tax preference

Green asset securitization will result in the transfer of assets, which is not only a financing action, but also a trading action, involving more complicated taxation issues than other green financial products and more intense demands on policy support （particularly tax preference policies）.

At present, green asset securitization has certain taxation burden issues in major sections, such as asset transfer, project benefit obtaining and circulation in secondary securities markets （analysis mainly from two aspects, i.e., income tax and VAT）. In terms of asset transfer, when the financiers transfer the basic assets to the entities with special purposes, they obtain the income specified in the *Enterprise Income Tax Law* and thus shall pay the enterprise income tax. For the transfer of receivables-type creditor assets, the existing taxation system does not specify whether or not to levy VAT and on what items for creditors' right assignment. In terms of obtaining project income, when financiers （playing the role of asset service institutions） get income from basic assets, VAT will be generated. When such income is paid by the asset service institutions to the entities with special purposes or by the entities with special purposes to investors, VAT will be generated respectively. In terms of secondary securities markets, the investors shall pay income taxes when trading green asset-backed securities, and pay VAT for the item as "transfer of financial product" as stipulated in the *Implementing Measures for Pilot of Change from Business Tax to Value-Added Tax*.

Green asset securitization requires the support from tax preference policies, which are specific means for a country to regulate the economy with taxation and play an important role in supporting the development of special industries. *The Guidelines on Constructing the Green Financial System* jointly released by seven ministries and commissions proposes to establish a complete green finance system, which requires the matching support of policies and relevant laws and regulations on finance, public finance and environmental protection. Therefore, the writer suggests that the relevant regulatory and taxation authorities for green asset securitization should jointly develop regulations specifying the taxation treatment rules on green asset securitization trading, and supporting the tax preference policies on green asset securitization, so as to reduce trading costs and fully mobilize the initiatives of the issuers, the asset management institutions and the investors to issue and purchase green asset-backed securities. Only the active participation of market players may stimulate the potential of green asset securitization market and promote the development of green finance and green industry.

（ii） Encourage dual-green projects and enrich asset types

Though the assets within green asset-backed securities are not limited to green projects, it is encouraged to issue asset-backed securities with green basic assets, so as to realize the "dual-green" sources and purposes. According to the asset-backed securities products already issued basic assets belong to green projects, but they are mainly concentrated in the right to earnings from sewage disposal charges, right to earnings from public transport operation charges, right to earnings from grid electricity charges and green loans, while the types of green projects are much more comprehensive than these. The *Climate Bond Standards* (CBS) developed by the Climate Bonds Initiative includes 44 types of green projects in 8 categories, while Chinese version of green standards, *Directory of Green Bonds-Backed Projects*, also includes 31 types of green projects in 6 categories. Therefore, in terms of green credit, the data released by CBRC indicates that as of the end of June 2016, the green credit balance of 21 major financial institutions in the banking sector reached RMB 7.26 trillion, accounting for 9.0% of all types of loans.[1] Therefore, the green credit asset securitization has a huge asset mass, while the actual released size is rather small. In theory, green asset-backed securities can be issued as long as green projects generate stable cash flow and project owners guarantee to raise capital for green projects. So it is suggested that the regulators should encourage market innovation, enrich the securitized basic asset types, and stimulate market potentials.

(iii) Encourage the combination of green asset securitization with PPP

The ordinary mode of public-private partnership (PPP) is that the social capital undertakes the majority of the work of infrastructure design, construction, operation and maintenance, and obtains reasonable investment returns through "user pays" and if necessary, "government pays". PPP is a major economic reform task determined by the country, which is of great significance for accelerating the construction of new urbanization, promoting the capacity of national governance, and constructing the modern fiscal system.

Most of the PPP projects already released currently involve green industry, including public charging facilities for new energy vehicle, sewage treatment works, sludge and kitchen (waste) treatment works, waste treatment facilities, ecological comprehensive improvements and landscaping. According to the *Analysis Report on the Third Batch of Demonstrative Projects* released by PPP Center under the Ministry of Finance, there are a total of 46 ecological construction and environmental protection projects, with a total investment value of RMB 81 billion, the number of projects accounting for 8.9%, and the total investment accounting for 6.9%.

However, due to the long return period in green industries, obstructed investor exit channels and more, the enthusiasm of private capital to invest in PPP projects is generally not high. Combining green asset securitization with the PPP model may better solve this problem: First, through asset securitization, the initiator may get the projects future cash flow of the project at one time, and meet the requirements of investors' instant exit from PPP projects (of course, according to the core of green asset securitization, the green, PPP project investors should commit to raise capital for other green projects). Second, asset securitization has flexible structures, the products with long duration could be issued, and it adapts to the characteristic of long return periods for PPP projects. Third, PPP projects have stable cash flows and are naturally suitable for securitization. Therefore, for green PPP projects, future cash flow may be realized in advance through asset

---

[1] www.ce.cn, CBRC: Green Credit Fueled Economic Restructuring http://finance.ce.cn/rolling/201609/03/t20160903_15551168. shtml, last accessed on December 1, 2017.

securitization, which may speed up the investors' capital recovery, thus attracting more social capital to participate in green industries[1]. For green asset securitization, the active participation in green PPP projects may not only provide capital to support green PPP projects, but also expand the size of green asset securitization and strengthen the recognition of asset securitization in the market. Therefore, the combination of green asset securitization with PPPs may effectively promote the development of green industries.

（iv） Encourage information disclosure and establish assessment rules

Currently, listed companies pay more and more attention to corporate social responsibilities （CSR）, and the author believes that participating in green finance should also be part of CSR. Therefore, the writer suggests that corresponding information disclosure rules should be established. Major participants in green finance such as listed companies （mainly including environmental polluting enterprises and enterprises engaged in green industry）, asset managers, and institutional investors should disclose the details of their participation in green finance, such as the basic information on the proportion of issued or invested products of the total finance products issued or invested by the disclosing participants. If not actively participating in green finance, such non-participation should also be specified. Meanwhile, the corresponding assessment rules should be established, and for the participants highlighting such disclosure, incentive measures such as setting rewards

and simplifying relevant review work may be considered.

Green finance is an important measure for introducing finance into green projects, which may promote industrial upgrading and development and meet environmental and public interest. Asset securitization is a flexible and accurate financing instrument that will further meet the capital demands of green industries and promote a rapid development in these sectors. Under the grand blueprint given in the report of the 19th CPC National Congress, China's green finance will be rejuvenated.

References:

[1] Analysis of Green Asset Securitization. China Finance Information Network, September 2, 2016.

[2] Cao Ping. Great Potential for Innovative Development of Green Asset Securitization, Securities Times, March 22, 2016.

[3] Chinese Academy for Environmental Planning.2016 Annual Report of China's Green Finance Policies[J]. Cai Zhidao, 2017 （8）.

[4] Hong Yanrong. International Rules and Implications of Green Bond Operation Mechanism[J]. Law Science, 2017 （2）.

[5] Ma Jun. Ten Fields of China's Green Finance Development[J].Wuhan Finance, 2017 （1）.

[6] Ma Jun. Development and Prospect of China's Green Finance[J]. Comparative Economic & Social Systems, 2016 （6）.

---

[1] xinhuanet.com, The Emergence of Green Asset Securitization Fuels Supply Side Reform, http://news.xinhuanet.com/finance/2016–03/03/c_128769279.htm, last accessed on December 1, 2017.

[7] PBOC Hangzhou Center Branch Office Group. Green Finance: International Experience, Inspiration and Countermeasures[J]. Money and Banking, 2011 （5）.

[8] Zhu Jin, Li Yongkun. Analysis of Asset Securitization Financing Modes in Green Industry and Intervention Modes of Financial Institutions[J]. Modern Management Science, 2017 （10）.

Table 1   Summarization of Green Asset-Backed Securities Products Already Issued[1]

No.	Name of product	Establishment day	Issuer	Basic asset	Issuing size (RMB 100 million)	Credit rating	Average issuing rate	Whether green assessment is performed (certification organization)	Whether labeling	Purpose of capital
1	Harvest Capital — CECEP Green Building Asset Supporting Special Plan	11/2/2017	China Energy Conservation and Environmental Protection Group	Chengdu International Technical Energy Conservation Building	8.20	AAA	5.20%	/	No	/
2	Nantong Economic and Technological Development Area Sewage Treatment Charging Right Green Asset Supporting Special Plan	9/15/2017	Nantong Economic and Technological Development Area Co., Ltd.	Sewage Treatment Charging Right	5.10	AA+	6.30%	Yes (Beijing Zhongcai Lvrong Consulting Co., Ltd.)	Yes	General environmental improvement (including waterway dredging) project
3	Tgood Receivables Phase I Green Asset Supporting Special Plan	9/14/2017	Qingdao Tgood Electric Co., Ltd.	Receivables creditor's rights	9.83	AAA AA A+	6.30%	/	No	Construction and operation of new energy vehicle charging facility projects

[1] Data sorted and summarized according to the information available in the Internet.

Continued table

No.	Name of product	Establishment day	Issuer	Basic asset	Issuing size (RMB 100 million)	Credit rating	Average issuing rate	Whether green assessment is performed (certification organization)	Whether labeling	Purpose of capital
4	Sound Water Beijing Phase I Green Asset Supporting Special Plan	8/23/2017	Beijing Yushun Environmental Protection Co., Ltd.	Sewage Treatment Charging Right	8.20	AA+	6.50%	Yes (Beijing SynTao Green Finance Consulting Co., Ltd.)	Yes	Repayment of financing lease debt, Shunyi Sewage Treatment Plant Phase II expansion project and Phase III expansion project construction
5	Gezhouba Lvyuan Green Receivables Phase I Asset Supporting Special Plan	8/10/2017	Gezhouba Huanjia (Dalian) Renewable Resources Co., Ltd. Gezhouba Xingye Renewable Resources Co., Ltd.	Receivables creditor's rights	13.04	AA+ AA	6.50%	/	Yes	/
6	China Investment Securities — Wuhan Metro Trust Beneficiary Right Phase I Green Asset Supporting Special Plan	7/18/2017	Wuhan Rail Transit Construction Co., Ltd.	Trust beneficiary right	15.00	AAA	5.07%	/	Yes	/

No.	Name of product	Establishment day	Issuer	Basic asset	Issuing size (RMB 100 million)	Credit rating	Average issuing rate	Whether green assessment is performed (certification organization)	Whether labeling	Purpose of capital
7	Ping'an — Guiyang Public Transport Operation Charging Right Green Asset Supporting Special Plan	3/29/2017	Guiyang Public Traffic Company	Public transport operation charging right	26.50	AAA	5.72%	Yes (Beijing Zhongcai Lvrong Consulting Co., Ltd.)	Yes	Construction and operation of Guiyang public traffic green industry projects
8	Huatai Asset Management — Gezhouba Grid Hydropower Charging Right Green Asset Supporting Special Plan	11/22/2016	China Gezhouba (Group) Corporation	Hydropower charging right	8.00	AAA	3.41%	Yes (Beijing Zhongcai Lvrong Consulting Co., Ltd.)	Yes	Re-financing of hydropower stations
9	Wuxi Transportation Industry Group Public Transport Operation Charging Right Green Asset Supporting Special Plan	9/28/2016	Wuxi Transportation Industry Group Co., Ltd.	Public transport operation charging right	19.80	AAA	3.72%	/	Yes	Purchase of public transport vehicles (focusing on new energy buses and clean energy buses) Operation of public transportation facilities
10	Nongyin Suiying — Goldwind Wind Power Charging Right Green Asset Supporting Special Plan	8/3/2016	Xinjiang Goldwind Science & Technology Co., Ltd.	Wind power charging right	12.75	AAA	3.92%	Yes (DET NORSKE VERITAS, IFC)	Yes	Repayment of the outstanding bank loans of project company, and supplementation to the working capital of the company or project company

Continued table

No.	Name of product	Establishment day	Issuer	Basic asset	Issuing size (RMB 100 million)	Credit rating	Average issuing rate	Whether green assessment is performed (certification organization)	Whether labeling	Purpose of capital
11	Jiashi Energy Conservation No. 1 Asset Supporting Special Plan	10/16/2015	China Energy Conservation and Environmental Protection Group	Charging right on power generation from combustion of municipal solid wastes	6.80	AAA	/	/	No	/
12	2016 Industrial Bank Phase I Green Credit Asset-Backed Securities	1/7/2016	Industrial Bank Co., Ltd.	Green loan	26.46	AAA, A+	3.56%	/	No	/
13	2014 Xingyuan Phase II Green Credit Asset-Backed Securities	9/18/2014	Industrial Bank Co., Ltd.	Green loan	34.94	AAA A+ /AA	5.50%	/	No	/
14	2017 SPIC Ronghe Financing Lease Phase I Green Asset Supporting Notes	6/29/2017	SPIC Ronghe Financing Lease Co., Ltd.	Lease of creditor's rights and other rights and collateral rights	24.84	AAA AA	/	Yes (China Chengxin International Credit Rating Co., Ltd.)	No	/
15	2017 Beijing Enterprises Water Group (China) Investment Limited Phase I Green Asset Supporting Notes	4/25/2017	Beijing Enterprises Water Group (China) Investment Limited	Sewage treatment charging right	21.00	AAA	5.03%	Yes (Beijing SynTao Green Finance Consulting Co., Ltd.)	No	Construction of green projects Supplementation of corporate working capital

加快绿色证券化进程

■ Michael Sheren[1]

摘要：目前全球保险公司、养老基金、主权财富基金和其他机构投资人管理下的资金总额将近100万亿美元，但绿色投资只占了不到1%。目前迫切需要一种能将可持续贷款从银行转移到资本市场的资金转移机制，而证券化正是这种机制。绿色证券化并非万能，但却是匹配长期投资人与长期可持续资产进而管理全球资产余额的重要工具。此外，实践证明其可持续投资表现更佳，并且相对其他投资来说违约率更低。

《巴黎气候协定》的签署传达出明确信号，即世界各国的当务之急是转变高碳、高污染和资源密集型的经济发展模式。快速推进转型，有助于缓解气候变化带来的负面影响，促进新型可持续经济的发展。可持续经济增长的范畴包含了从可持续基础设施到创新电池技术，并将推动面向未来的新工作。但是，以特定速度为可持续经济发展提供特定额度的融资，难度很大，需恢复并加快全球债券资本市场发行绿色证券化债券的进程。

证券化[2]是一把双刃剑，它一方面可能导致金融危机，另一方面却又是全球债权资本市场的重要工具，有助于银行腾出资产余额，以向资本市场出售资产的形式，获得更高额度的贷款。标准化债务产品能够重新包装成资产担保证券，如车贷和信用应收账款；更高额度、更复杂的债务，如杠杆贷款，转让后可变为贷款抵押债券。在金融危机发生时和金融危机过后，除美国个人住房抵押贷款支持证券（RMBS）外，绝大多数这类贷款都运行良好[3]。但是，证券化都会受美国次级RMBS影响，导致市场"紧急刹车"，并且在证券化过程中导致全球金融系统衰退。截至2017年第三季度，房利美已印发230亿美元绿色住宅抵押贷款，但RMBS还在等待借款人偿还资金，全球证券化市场的复苏过程非常缓慢。虽然当前证券化市场名声已经受损，但却仍然蓄势待发。重新审视、架构和加快证券化进程的时机已经成熟，推进绿色证券化有助于发挥其在保护地

---

[1] Michal Sheren系中央财经大学绿色金融国际研究院学术委员会联合主席。
[2] 证券化的定义包括：资产证券、抵押债券和资产担保债券、住宅/商业抵押贷款支持证券等。
[3] https://www.spratings.com/documents/20184/1393097/SF10Years/b0f1300a-5ed5-407d-8d3b-77fdc3b1f20c.

球、抵御气候变化中应有的作用。

全球经济向绿色经济转型同样需要大量资金，未来15年，仅可持续基础设施建设就需要90万亿美元资金[1]。目前，大多数基础设施建设和其他资产，可以通过银行贷款的方式筹集资金，如电动汽车和绿色抵押贷款[2]。经济转型融资是一项非常庞大的工程，单靠商业银行的资金支持恐难以实现[3]。此外，许多可持续项目投资要求期限较长，通常还要求固定利率和按需存取的存款，其中前者与批发贷款的短期浮动期限贷款不匹配，而后者就会成为银行余额。由此可见，流动性较高的债务资本市场才是可持续发展方案需要特别重视的环节。为新型可持续发展公司和资产释放出资产余额，需将流动性较差的银行贷款重新以流动的形式进行重新配置，以吸引长期投资者。

目前全球保险公司、养老基金、主权财富基金和其他机构投资人管理下的资金总额将近100万亿美元[4]，但绿色投资只占了不到1%[5]。大多数机构投资人只能购买如债券等公开发行、定额且可自由交易的投资产品。银行贷款大多数都达不到机构投资人的投资标准，但重新配置后的贷款可以，因此，放开数万亿经过流动性调整的资金可为经济转型提供资金。目前，迫切需要一种能将可持续贷款从银行转移到资本市场的资金转移机制，而证券化正是发挥这种作用的机制。

2016年共发行绿色债券951亿美元[6]，而其中只有75亿美元为资产抵押债券[7]。虽说过去五年绿色债券的总额不断增长，但是对于体量为90万亿美元[8]的全球债券市场来说，绿色债券只占了极小部分[9]。为增加交易流量并且实现图1列出的目标，需加快从银行资产余额到资本市场的证券化步伐。这样一来，不仅绿色资产可以转移给机构投资人，而且也会让银行释放出更多资金，承销更高额度的绿色贷款。由此，也将促进资金回流，创建一个绿色的循环。

---

[1] http://newclimateeconomy.report/2016/.

[2] http://cfi.co/finance/2017/07/otaviano-canuto-world-bank-matchmaking-finance-and-infrastructure/；IJGlobal 和 Thomson One Banker的统计数据显示，2007–2015年66%–90%的全球项目资金来自银行贷款。来源：2016年第一季度排名分析报告（2016年4月15日），IJGlobal；国际金融项目，Thomson One Banker。

[3] 全球最大银行的总余额不足以支撑可持续基础设施建设所需的90万亿美元。 http://www.snl.com/web/client?auth=inherit#news/article?id=40223698&cdid=A-40223698-11568.

[4] http://www.worldbank.org/en/news/feature/2015/06/18/institutional-investors-the-unfulfilled-100-trillion-promise.

[5] http://www.oecd.org/cgfi/resources/Progress_Report_on_Approaches_to_Mobilising_Institutional_Investment_for_Green_Infrastructure.pdf.

[6] https://about.bnef.com/blog/green-bonds-2016-review/.

[7] SEB & Bloomberg.

[8] http://europe.pimco.com/EN/Education/Pages/Everythingyouneedtoknowaboutbonds.aspx.

[9] 截至2017年1月，累计发行绿色债券总额为2210亿美元；虽说占全球债券市场92.7万亿美元的比例非常小（0.25%），但发展迅速。2017年第一季度绿色债券发行量占全球债务资本市场成效总额的2.1%，年增长率1.4%。资料来源：SEB & Bloomberg。

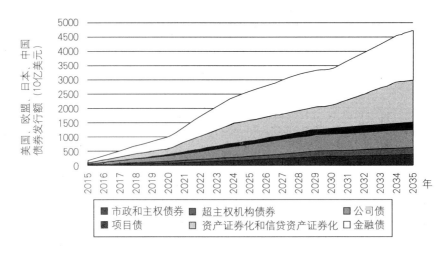

■ 市政和主权债券	■ 超主权机构债券	▨ 公司债
■ 项目债	▨ 资产证券化和信贷资产证券化	□ 金融债

资料来源：OECD（2016），低碳转型中债券影响因素分析[1]。

图1　到2030年，绿色资产抵押债券/贷款抵押债券年发行量有望达到2800亿-3800亿美元

通过银行资产负债表上已确认和已标记的贷款金额，可以衡量证券化对绿色金融的促进作用。标记为绿色贷款的贷款符合绿色证券化要求，如果绿色贷款已确认、标记、合并，需对证券进行结构化调整，以满足全球机构投资人的不同投资偏好。必要的结构化工作主要是为获得理想的信用评级、期限、汇率和优惠，以便最大限度地提高流动性，当然这些只是投资偏好中的一部分。个别情况下，债券可能不能达到一个或者多个所需偏好，在这种情况下，可使用金融结构工具。金融结构工具包括信用分组、第一损失担保、保险和超额担保，但同时不能夸大此类工具的重要性，也不能过度强调此类工具通过债券结构化吸引私人机构投资人资本挤入、提高流动性的作用。

新兴市场以债券结构化吸引国际机构投资人的做法可能为国家风险、流动性较低的货币和法律规则带来另外的挑战。但是，可以借助金融结构化工具为新兴市场资产抵押绿色债券提供支持。其中，最重要的工具是创建次级债务，在发生违约的情况下，可以为优先债务提供第一损失担保。通过次级债务结构化为部分债券投保或提供担保，可以提升债券优先债务的信用等级，进而吸引私有部门投资者。此外，绿色金融风险第一损失担保可以削减资本成本，这样银行就可以承销更高额度的绿色贷款，只要让银行在贷款中持续获得利益就可以构建互利联盟。

监管方面，证券化复苏已取得巨大进展，不过挑战依然存在。欧盟正在积极构建简单、透明、标准化资产证券化产品（STS），并将其作为资金要求较低、更健全也更安全的资产类别。但是，欧盟内的大多数保险公司仍被排除在证券化之外，因为他们与欧盟偿付能力指引II的资本要求相冲突。在美国，定义真实出售资格的风险自留规则在会计处理过程中会暴露清晰度不足的缺点，并且可能引发市场混乱。这类问题的清晰度对增加欧盟和美国的绿色证券化规模有着非凡意义。因此，对市场来说，确定和调整可持续基础设施建设领域与证券监管之间的冲突是积极信号。

---

[1] http://www.oecd.org/cgfi/quantitative-framework-bond-contributions-in-a-low-carbon-transition.pdf.

绿色证券化并非万能，但却是匹配长期投资人与长期可持续资产，进而管理全球资产余额的重要工具。此外，实验证明，绿色证券化可持续投资表现更佳，且相对于其他投资来说，违约率更低[1]。因此，对全球来说，向可持续经济转型融资非常重要，它本身也是一种理性投资。银行仍然站在可持续项目融资的最前沿，基础设施建设是绿色化发展中资金需求最大的领域。因此，加速绿色贷款进入债务资本市场是推动转型和为机构投资人提供长期资产的重要工具。但是，绿色证券化又有别于其他融资方案，它有助于银行签发绿色贷款，加快投入绿色金融的资本回流。

针对巨大挑战，需大刀阔斧、突破陈规的解决方案。目前，没有什么问题比气候变化对人类的威胁更严重，支持加快绿色证券化发展是解决方案的一部分。绿色证券化是实现推动绿色资本市场发展万亿美元融资需求的重要一步，将推动世界走上可持续发展的道路。

（Michael Sheren现任中央财经大学绿色金融国际研究院学术委员会联合主席，从事债务资本市场相关工作25年，先后就职于伦敦和纽约。本文谨代表个人观点，不代表Michael Sheren所在组织的政策或观点。）

---

[1] http://www.oecd.org/cgfi/quantitative-framework-bond-contributions-in-a-low-carbon-transition.pdf.

Accelerating Green Securitisation

■ Michael Sheren[1]

Abstract: Globally, there is nearly $US 100 trillion under management between insurance companies, pension funds, sovereign wealth funds and other institutional investors; however, currently less than 1% of their holdings are in green investments. A transfer mechanism to move sustainable loans from banks to the capital markets is needed and securitisation is that mechanism. Green securitisation is not a silver bullet but it is an important tool to manage the global balance sheet by matching long term investors with long terms sustainable assets. Further, empirical evidence is emerging that sustainable investments perform better and default less than other investments.

The message sent following the ratification of the Paris Agreement on climate change was clear, the world must urgently transit away from a high carbon, polluting and resource intensive economic model. Rapidly advancing this transition should help mitigate the worst effects of climate change and facilitate new sustainable economic growth. This growth will range from sustainable infrastructure to innovative battery technology and act as an engine for new future *facing j*obs. However, financing these opportunities at the necessary *scale and pace* will be more difficult without reviving and then *accelerating* the issuance of green securitised bonds within the global debt capital markets.

Leading up to the financial crisis, securitisation[2] was an important work-horse within the global debt capital markets helping banks to free up balance sheet to underwrite more loans by selling assets in to the capital markets. Standardised debt products such as car loans and credit card receivables were repackaged into asset based securities. Larger and more complex debt such as

---

[1] Michael Sheren, Co-Chair of the Academic Michal Sheren, Co-Chair of the International Institute of Green Finance at the Central University of Finance and Economics, Beijing China.

[2] Securitisation defined across all pooling structures: asset based securities, collateralised debt obligations and covered bonds, residential/commercial mortgage backed securities etc.

leveraged loans were sold into collateralised loan obligations. Other than US residential mortgage backed securities（"RMBS"）, the vast majority of these pooled structures held up very well during and after the financial crisis[1]. However, all securitisation was tainted by the US sub-prime RMBS that brought the market to a screeching halt and in the process, almost took down the global financial system. That said, even RMBS is looking for redemption as Fannie Mae has printed $US 23 billion worth of green residential mortgages as of Q3 2017. The recovery of the global securitisation market has been slow. However, it is gaining momentum and despite its tarnished reputation, it's time to re-exam, restructure and accelerate securitisation so it can play its part in saving the planet from climate change.

The amount of capital needed to finance the green transition in the global economy is staggering; over the next fifteen years sustainable Infrastructure alone will demand over $90 trillion.[2] Currently most infrastructure and other assets such as electric vehicles and green mortgages are funded by bank loans[3]. The enormous task of financing the transition is too big to be achieved solely off the backs of commercial banks[4]. Further, many sustainable investments require long tenors, often fixed rate that are miss-matched with the short-term floating tenors of wholesale borrowing and on-demand deposits that make up bank balance sheets. Hence, the highly liquid debt capital markets must be major part of the sustainable solution. To release balance sheet capacity for new sustainable companies and assets, illiquid bank loans must be repackaged into a liquid format that appeals to long term investors.

Globally, there is nearly $US 100 trillion[5] under management between insurance companies, pension funds, sovereign wealth funds and other institutional investors; however, currently less than 1%[6] of their holdings are in green investments. Most institutional investors can only purchase public, rated and freely tradable investment products such as bonds. Bank loans largely do not meet the investment criteria of institutional investors; however, repackaged loans qualify, thereby opening up trillions of new liquidity to fund the transition. A transfer mechanism to move sustainable loans from banks to the capital markets is needed and securitisation is that mechanism.

In 2016, a total of $US 95.1[7] billion of green bonds were issued but only $US 7.5 billion of this volume was ABS[8] Despite a continued

---

[1] https://www.spratings.com/documents/20184/1393097/SF10Years/b0f1300a–5ed5–407d–8d3b–77fdc3b1f20c.

[2] http://newclimateeconomy.report/2016/.

[3] http://cfi.co/finance/2017/07/otaviano–canuto–world–bank–matchmaking–finance–and–infrastructure/ ; According to IJGlobal and Thomson One Banker, 66%–90% of global project finance are funded by bank loans from 2007–2015. Sources: Q1 2016 League table Analysis （April 15 2016）, IJGlobal; Project Financial International, Thomson One Banker.

[4] Total on balance sheet assets of the world's largest banks are less than the $US 90 trillion needed just for sustainable infrastructure http://www.snl.com/web/client?auth=inherit#news/article?id=40223698&cdid=A–40223698–11568.

[5] http://www.worldbank.org/en/news/feature/2015/06/18/institutional–investors–the–unfulfilled–100–trillion–promise.

[6] http://www.oecd.org/cgfi/resources/Progress_Report_on_Approaches_to_Mobilising_Institutional_Investment_for_Green_Infrastructure.pdf.

[7] https://about.bnef.com/blog/green–bonds–2016–review/.

[8] SEB & Bloomberg.

increase in volume over the last five years, green bonds of all types remain a small fraction[1] of the $US 90[2] trillion global bond markets. To increase deal flow and achieve the potential volumes calculated in Figure 1, the securitised path from bank balance sheets to the capital markets must be accelerated. In doing so, not only will green assets migrate to institutional investors, bank balances will be freed up to underwrite NEW green loans. Thereby recycling the funds and creating a green circle.

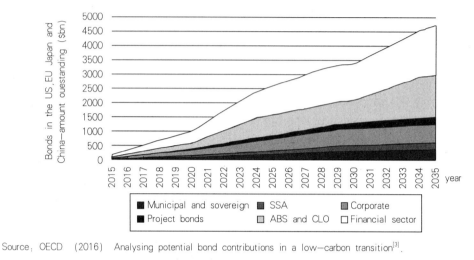

Source: OECD (2016) Analysing potential bond contributions in a low-carbon transition[3].

Figure 1   Green ABS/CLO has the potential to scale to USD 280–380 billion in annual issuance by 2030

Accelerating green finance through securitisation would see banks, in scale, identifying and tagging eligible loans on their balance sheets. Loans tagged as green would be eligible for green securitisation. Once the green loans are identified, tagged and pooled, the securities would be structured to meet the investment preferences of global institutional investors. Essential structuring work would aim to obtain an optimal credit rating, tenor, currency and coupon, among other investment preferences to maximise liquidity. In some cases, a bond may not achieve one or more of the desired preferences and in such cases, financial structuring tools could be employed. These tools include credit tranching, first loss guarantees, insurance and over-collateralisation. The importance of these tools and their ability to attract liquidity by structuring bonds in a way that crowds-in private institutional investors cannot be overstated.

Structuring bonds to attract international institutional investors in emerging markets can pose challenges around country risk, illiquid currencies and rule of law. However, some of the financial structuring tools mentioned

---

[1] Total cumulative green bond issuance stood at USD 221 billion as of January 2017; a minute but rapidly growing fraction (0.25%) of the USD 92.7 trillion global bond markets. Green bond issuance accounted for 2.1% of global debt capital markets underwriting volume in 1Q17 up from 1.4% YoY. Source: SEB & Bloomberg.

[2] http://europe.pimco.com/EN/Education/Pages/Everythingyouneedtoknowaboutbonds.aspx.

[3] http://www.oecd.org/cgfi/quantitative-framework-bond-contributions-in-a-low-carbon-transition.pdf.

above can be applied to support asset based green bonds in these markets. The most important tool is creating a subordinated portion of debt that will take the first loss over the senior debt in the event of default. By structuring a subordinated tranche or by providing insurance or a guarantee over a portion of the bond, the credit of the senior portion of the bond is enhanced and can bring in private sector investors. Further, transferring the first loss or guaranteeing this risk in respect of green financing will reduce the capital to allow the bank to originate more green loans. Alignment of interests can be achieved through a requirement that originating banks retain an ongoing interest in the loans.

On the regulatory side, there has been significant progress in reviving securitisation, however, challenges persist. In the EU, efforts to structure Simple Transparent and Standardised (STS) securitisation as a stronger and safer asset class that would carry lower capital requirements is progressing. However, EU Insurance companies remain mostly locked out of securitisations by challenging capital requirements under Solvency II. In the US, lack of clarity on the accounting treatment on risk retention rules that define what qualifies as a true sale have surfaced causing confusion in the market. Clarity on these issues could meaningfully increase the volume of green securitisation in the EU and United States. Finally, an effort to identify and adjust the regulatory friction to securities in areas around sustainable infrastructure would be a positive signal to the markets.

Green securitisation is not a silver bullet but it is an important tool to manage the global balance sheet by matching long term investors with long terms sustainable assets. Further, empirical evidence is emerging that sustainable investments perform better and default less than other investments[1]. Hence, financing the transition to a sustainable world is not just essential for the planet, it's also smart investing. Banks remain on the front line of financing sustainable projects and infrastructure represents the biggest need for green growth; therefore, the acceleration of green loans to the debt capital markets is essential to drive the transition and provide long terms assets to institutional investors. But, green securitisation, unlike the other financing solutions above, allows banks that originate green loans to recycle the capital they dedicate to green financing.

A big challenge calls for big, bold action. There is no challenge bigger than the threat to humanity posed by climate change. Support for the accelerated development of green securitisation should be part of the solution. This initiative could be an important step in moving the trillions required by growing a sustainable global green capital markets product of scale that will help put the world on the path to a sustainable future.

Michael Sheren is the Co-Chair of the Academic Committee of the International Institute of Green Finance at the Central University of Finance and Economics, Beijing China. Mr. Sheren spent over twenty-five years in the debt capital markets in London and New York. This article was written in a personal capacity and does not reflect the policies or opinions of any organisation affiliated with Mr. Sheren.

---

[1] https://www.bofaml.com/content/dam/boamlimages/documents/articles/ID17_0028/equityStrategyFocusPointADeeperDive.pdf.

绿色金融的国际趋势与中国的领导地位

■ Scott Vaughan[1]

摘要：中国绿色金融的创新速度确实令人瞩目。许多国家和机构都在研究中国在绿色金融这一关键领域的领导地位。中国不断试行新政策并建立绿色金融改革创新试验区来检验创新政策，这无论对中国还是对世界来说都有着非常重要的意义。

一、前言：生态文明

中国共产党第十九次全国代表大会标志着一个重要转折点，会上总结了中国在环境保护、污染治理、气候变化减缓和适应领域不断加强的领导地位，并提出了更广泛的生态文明框架。中国国家主席习近平在报告中强调了生态文明建设的重要性：

生态文明制度体系加快形成，主体功能区制度逐步健全，国家公园体制试点积极推进。全面节约资源有效推进，能源资源消耗强度大幅下降。重大生态保护和修复工程进展顺利，森林覆盖率持续提高。生态环境治理明显加强，环境状况得到改善。引导应对气候变化国际合作，成为全球生态文明建设的重要参与者、贡献者、引领者。

与生态文明概念相关的创新涉及多个领域，绿色金融是重点创新领域之一。

30年来，我们一直关注金融服务部门的绿色化问题。上世纪80年代末，一些银行已实行内部环境风险调查政策，其中包括德意志银行、加拿大皇家银行金融集团等。1992年，在联合国环境规划署工作期间，本人联合银行几位同事共同发起联合国环境规划署金融体系探寻项目。多年来，绿色金融相关工作一直未间断。自2015年以来，绿色金融一直保持良好的发展势头，且具有深远的政策参考意义。随着《巴黎气候协定》和《可持续发展目标》的签署，讨论主题从价值数十亿美元的污染防治和其他问题转移到价值数万亿美元纳入核心环境和可持续发展标准的金融体

---

[1] Scott Vaughan，国际可持续发展研究院首席执行官兼院长。

系上来。这就是常说的"数十亿到数万亿"转型，议题也不再是绿色金融发展初期关于小型项目融资的讨论，如今的议题目标更高远，转而围绕推进系统性改革以构建有助于实现可持续发展目标的金融体系展开讨论。

二、绿色金融在中国

绿色金融在中国推行已有十年。2017年谢孟哲和王遥发表报告《构建中国绿色金融体系》，总结了各方面创新的进展情况，如监管改革、绿色债券。中国处于领导地位的主要特色是强调政策的前后一贯性，多个国家机构协作配合中国绿色金融系统性发展，如中国人民银行、中国银行业监督管理委员会、中国保险监督管理委员会等主要负责协调规则、市场信号、风险工具和创新产品的关系。中国共产党第十八届中央委员会第三次全体会议着重强调了上述模式，指出"必须建立系统完整的生态文明制度体系，用制度保护生态环境"。

2014年生态文明贵阳国际论坛上，中国绿色金融工作正式宣布启动，这是中国绿色金融元年。生态文明国际论坛是中国国家级国际论坛，来自中国与国际的专家围绕一系列生态问题交流探讨，如节能环保、大数据，并成立绿色金融工作小组，确定了中方与外方专家召集人。

工作小组的工作任务令人瞩目，内容涵盖广泛，目标高远。中国人民银行副行长指出，工作小组不仅可识别可杜绝生态危害的绿色金融发展模式，且能确定为绿色投资提供支持的金融产品和实践。环境风险和机遇统筹兼顾是联合国环境规划署金融体系探寻项目关注的工作重点。工作小组议程涉及众多主要监管机构和金融机构，如中国银行业监督管理委员会、财政部、兴业银行，因此，工作小组计划性地将工作议程分多个层次，同时也注重各层次间的交叉混合。工作小组的工作范畴广泛，包含绿色银行、绿色债券、

绿色保险、绿色IPO、绿色信贷评级、银行环境负债、绿色信息披露、绿色数据库、绿色投资人网络、中国对外绿色投资、绿色资产证券化、银行环境风险生态恢复力测试及鼓励中国国内银行采用实施赤道原则等。

三、利用现有产品、新产品和混合融资

2015年，工作小组发布报告《构建中国绿色金融体系》。报告特别强调实际成果，针对所有研究主题详细介绍了一系列具体行动，并提出相应建议。此外，马骏博士还指出推进中国绿色金融体系建设必备的六个重要原则：

1. 在限制污染性投资措施基础上，有更多激励绿色投资机制；

2. 通过现有银行渠道推动绿色信贷，同时考虑推动成立新的专业性绿色贷款与投资机构；

3. 减少对行政命令的依赖，更多使用财政金融等手段，通过市场机制激励社会资金投向绿色行业；

4. 推动绿色贷款，同时发展绿色债券、绿色股票、绿色基金、绿色保险、碳交易等多种绿色融资渠道和金融产品；

5. 该体系应通过公共资金和法律杠杆撬动和加速私人资本投资。在2015年的亚的斯亚贝巴金融发展峰会上，强调了通过混合手段推动绿色金融发展的重要性。这样的方式可以避免增加公共资金压力，并撬动更多的资金投入到绿色产业当中。马骏博士也曾指出，政府的政策信号可以引导投资行为中的资金流动。

6. 支持绿色投资，与此同时，为绿色投资提供金融基础设施，包括建立帮助投资者评估项目环境影响的方法和数据库、绿色评级和环境信息披露规制。只有提高环境信息和成本的可获得性，绿色金融通过市场机制引导绿色投资的作用才能得到有效发挥。

以上六个主要原则对现有机构和机制设置提

供了非常宝贵的路线图，同时以创新为驱动扩展新产品，如绿色债券。

四、中国在G20绿色金融各项工作中的领导地位

基于2015年工作小组发布的报告《构建中国绿色金融体系》，中国在担任G20轮值主席国期间，推动建立G20绿色金融研究小组，由中国人民银行和英格兰银行共同主持，联合国环境规划署（UNEP）担任秘书处。G20绿色金融研究小组的工作任务是"识别绿色金融发展所面临的体制和市场障碍，并在总结各国经验的基础上，提出可提升金融体系动员私人部门绿色投资能力的可选措施"。

2016年，G20绿色金融研究小组提出系列工作目标，包括着重强调的扩展特定新产品，如绿色债券，提高绿色金融自愿原则的普及，加强环境风险信息披露以及分担金融服务部门普遍存在的系统性风险。为此，G20研究小组建议明确战略政策信号和框架，特别是《可持续发展目标》和《巴黎协议》，告知投资者投资趋势正向更清洁、更环保的低碳项目转型[1]。

五、进展与未来发展

在2017年9月纽约举办的联合国气候周会议上，一家全球性投资银行CEO在世界经济论坛会议上提出金融行业目前正处于向低碳和零碳排放转型的"拐点"。2017年11月，估价约1万亿美元的挪威主权财富基金宣布抛售其所持有的全部石油和天然气股份，以降低因"石油天然气价格持续下跌"带来的财务风险，这一做法无疑印证

了这一说法。早在2016年，该基金会就通过决议撤销对50多家煤炭企业的投资。关于煤炭的决策是基于基金会内部道德观和企业社会责任准则做出的，而石油和天然气决策则是完全基于经济分析做出的，分析结果显示石油和天然气部门的投资回报不断缩水。

六、转变市场与加强信息披露

当前，面临的重要问题是挪威基金的决定将对投资者和市场产生怎样的影响？国际可再生能源机构（IRENA）的分析结果显示，过去十年可再生能源融资额度呈大幅增长，不排除增长比例的波动，而传统能源资源仍存在较大的资金缺口。传统能源与清洁能源之间的资金差距由多方面原因造成，包括仍在实行的以支持化石燃料消费和生产的化石燃料补贴。据国际可持续发展研究所全球补贴研究中心（GSI）统计，每年补贴超过4000亿美元，相当于可再生能源价格补贴总额的四倍。

结合2015年工作小组发布的报告《构建中国绿色金融体系》和2016年G20议题中提出的绿色金融系统性框架分析挪威基金的做法，其不会造成市场波动；结合其他举措来看，绿色金融的强势发展势头不断凸显。2017年7月，金融稳定委员会（FSB）发布工作小组报告——《气候相关金融信息披露》，标志着绿色金融发展向前迈进了一大步。该报告涵盖了金融服务行业所有相关主体，呼吁披露实际和潜在的气候相关风险，建议建立衡量和对比风险的明确指标体系及可缓解上述风险的内部应对策略。

与此同时，金融稳定委员会（FSB）接受工作小组建议，并委托其继续开展工作。紧接着，

---

[1] "制定战略政策信号和框架：国家机关应针对绿色投资战略框架（比如想加入《可持续发展目标》和《巴黎协议》）面向投资人释放更明确的环境和经济政策信号。"

贝莱德和Vanguard等大型私人投资集团已注意到自身在加强气候风险披露方面的举措。中期，工作小组将重新定义与气候风险相关的重要性，反过来也为近380个强制性和自愿性企业报告平台的气候风险信息汇总提供了机会。

七、创新型绿色产品

2015年马骏博士指出，识别、披露和管理气候风险仍保持发展势头，但若要让绿色投资形成积极的发展势头需具有可比性。绿色投资显著发展的领域当属绿色债券，实现了飞速发展：如今，中国已成为全球绿色债券的最大发行国，法国和美国紧随其后。2017年11月，据穆迪统计，绿色债券总额达到950亿美元，相比去年增长近50%。为确保绿色债券的持续增长和合法性，需通过研究以明确绿色债券和纯债券的环境效益和影响，并确定不同债券发行方之间的对比指标。

到目前为止，可持续发展国际研究所对中国绿色金融的研究覆盖了绿色债券设计和发行、绿色证券化和税务处理等领域，助力扩展绿色投资，进而巩固中国在绿色金融领域的领导地位。如果经济绿色化总融资额中社会资金比例占85%，那么绿色债券会在公私混合融资中促进向绿色经济转型方面发挥越来越重要的作用。

绿色债券杠杆面临的一个挑战是将债券发行与项目规模挂钩。可持续发展国际研究所报告指出，机构投资者寻求发行规模超过2亿美元的债券，而市场更倾向于发行规模超过10亿美元乃至更大的债券。而在中国，债券发行规模一般在1亿美元以下，许多绿色项目，如绿色基础设施建设、综合水资源管理、重新造林和气候相关碳封存信用额度，项目规模可能还低于1亿美元的最低限额。实现潜在融资与项目所需资金相挂钩的一个方法是将小型项目进行捆绑，如以资产抵押证券形式捆绑。但项目捆绑反过来又会为衡量绿色债券和纯债券环境效益工作带来其他问题。与此同时，可持续发展国际研究所在报告中列出了其他挑战和可行方案，见下表。

挑战	可行方案
小规模项目和没有聚合因素的项目不利于满足债券发行规模的要求	绿色债券化：包括使用标准化贷款合同和金融仓储
潜在绿色债券发行方的信用评级较低，不利于吸引机构投资者	信用增级和绿色债券化
绿色项目的信用评级较低，不利于吸引机构投资者	信用增级
需增加绿色债券投资，以满足绿色债券扩大发行量的需求	绿色债券税收激励机制，包括绿色资产支持证券

绿色债券发行规模不断扩大，纳入绿色属性的金融产品创新层出不穷。近日，美国花旗集团发行效率服务协议（ESA），其在设计上与广泛使用的购电协议相似，旨在为可再生能源项目进行融资。ESA支持能源效率融资，本质上是通过效率升级就可实现的能源应用形式，不需要开展融资，如LED照明系统。2017年秋天，能源效率试点项目正式启动，预计花旗集团及其合作伙伴会将其打造成美国国内普遍使用的产品。

八、信号与框架

每周都会出现响应《巴黎协议》的创新金融产品发布。绿色金融产品创新持续推进，G20建议金融行业参考更广泛的政策信号和框架，如可持续发展目标（SDGs）。目前，SDGs处于实施初级阶段，国家层面上继续保持着良好的发展势头，包括主要私有部门主体及更广泛意义上的国际体系。SDGs主要基本特征强调全面综合的政

策措施，这样的政策行为较之于独立的专项措施效果更佳；面对迫在眉睫的全球生态退化、系统经济不确定性（如多边贸易体系）及各种社会问题（如国内或国际收入不平等），强调以转型变革作为解决方案。就其本身而论，SDGs被称为21世纪的新"布雷顿森林体系"。

中国推动制定的新型经济框架涉及标准经济衡量过程的指标改革，比如国内生产总值（GDP）。虽说GDP是迄今为止知道的人最多的指标，其目标并不是衡量相对于特定资产价值和收入流的增量。GDP的定义并不全面，其衡量的对象不是主要生态价值或污染损害的成本（除了修复相关的收支），也不是人类发展或集体利益等指标。GDP也无法预测将来的风险信号。

除了GDP外还有许多计算方法，包括参考剑桥大学经济学家达斯古普塔爵士等人开发的经济模型、数据和方法并依照联合国环境规划署包容性财富方法计算得出的全球数据。2016年，首份由IISD牵头，并基于联合国环境规划署全球项目研究成果的分析报告《加拿大综合财富报告》发布。该报告通过收入流情况，衡量可以反映真实财富的四大资本要素——人力资本、自然资本、技能资本和社会资本，以分析一个国家（加拿大）的全国进步发展情况。该报告成果展现出了与GDP数据截然不同的发展态势。例如，该报告展示了加拿大的自然资本在过去30年里下降了25%，这就释放出一个明确的政策信号，加拿大（可能也适用于其他依赖自然资源的国家）将来不可能重复过去的经济发展轨迹。《报告》以基础数据、数据分析和明确的方法学为依据，给出了与加拿大的预期发展模式和模型相反的发展依据。

这样的研究框架可以为绿色投资的增长，创造更为宽广的经济环境。当前，中国不以GDP作为发展的唯一衡量指标，反映了中国致力于开展整合性、前瞻性和创新性政策的决心。

九、结语

中国绿色金融的创新速度确实令人瞩目。许多国家和机构都在研究中国在绿色金融这一关键领域的领导地位。中国不断试行新政策并建立绿色金融改革创新试验区来检验创新政策。2017年6月，中国国务院宣布在浙江、江西、广东、贵州和新疆等地区建立绿色金融改革创新试验区，并根据试验区的发展管理总结特别是不同地区差异化试点的经验，这无论对中国还是对世界来说都有着非常重要的意义。

参考文献

[1]金融稳定委员会，工作小组针对环境相关金融信息披露的建议总结报告，2017，https://www.fsb-tcfd.org/wp-content/uploads/2017/06/FINAL-TCFD-Report-062817.pdf.

[2]G20绿色金融研究小组，G20绿色金融综合报告，2016，http://unepinquiry.org/wp-content/uploads/2016/09/Synthesis_Report_Full_EN.pdf.

[3]国际可持续发展研究所，综合财富报告，2017，http://www.iisd.org/comprehensivewealth/en/.

[4]中央财经大学绿色金融国际研究院和联合国环境规划署，2017，构建中国绿色金融体系：进展报告2017.

[5]http://unepinquiry.org/wpcontent/uploads/2017/11/China_Green_Finance_Progress_Report_2017_Summary.pdf.

[6]国际货币基金组织，2015，从数十亿到数万亿：多边开发金融机构2015年后金融转型发展规划；IMF。http://siteresources.worldbank.org/DEVCOMMINT/Documentation/23659446/DC2015-0002（E）FinancingforDevelopment.pdf.

[7]国际可再生能源机构，未注明出版日期，

金融和投资http://www.irena.org/financeinvestment.

[8]习近平，2017，决胜全面建成小康社会夺取新时代中国特色社会主义伟大胜利，中国共产党第十九次全国代表大会。http://www.xinhuanet.com/english/download/Xi_Jinping's_report_at_19th_CPC_National_Congress.pdf.

[9]Metrus Energy融资服务公司，2017，Metrus完成新财富100强技术公司委托的大型效率即服务项目。http://blog.metrusenergy.com/metrus-closes-massive-efficiency-as-a-service-project-for-new-fortune-100-technology-customer/.

[10]中国人民银行和联合国环境规划署，2015，构建中国绿色金融体系：中国绿色金融工作小组总结报告。

[11]http://unepinquiry.org/wpcontent/uploads/2015/12/Establishing_Chinas_Green_Financial_System_Final_Report.pdf.

[12]Weihui, Dai、Sean Kidney和Beate Sonerud，2016，中国路线图：借助绿色证券化、税收激励政策和信用增级扩大绿色债券；IISD和气候债券倡议组织。

International Trends of Green Finance and China's Leadership

■ Scott Vaughan[1]

Abstract: The pace of innovation in China in supporting green finance is indeed impressive. Many countries and institutions are now looking to Chinese leadership on this critical issue. China continues to pilot both new policies as well as pilot zones to test them. The lessons that emerge from these pilot zones, particularly in realizing a coherent system to accelerate green are of critical importance both for China and the world.

I. Introduction: Ecological Civilization

The 19th Congress of China marks an important moment in which China's leadership in environmental protection, pollution abatement, climate mitigation and adaptation work continue to grow, with a broader framework of ecological civilization.

In his report to the 19th Congress, China's President Xi Jinping framed the importance of the ecological civilization thus:

Efforts to develop a system for building an ecological civilization have been accelerated; the system of functional zoning has been steadily improved; and progress has been made in piloting the national park system. Across-the-board efforts to conserve resources have seen encouraging progress; the intensity of energy and resource consumption has been significantly reduced. Smooth progress has been made in major ecological conservation and restoration projects; and forest coverage has been increased. Ecological and environmental governance has been significantly strengthened, leading to marked improvements in the environment. Taking a driving seat in international cooperation

---
[1] Scott Vaughan, CEO and President of International Institute for Sustainable Development.

to respond to climate change, China has become an important participant, contributor, and torchbearer in the global endeavor for ecological civilization.

Among the key areas of accelerating innovation related to the concept of Ecological Civilization is green finance.

Interest in greening the financial services sector has existed for three decades, with some banks – including Deutsche Bank, RBF Financial Group and others – adopting some internal environmental risk screening policies in the late 1980s. In 1992, while working at UNEP, I worked with colleagues from a small group of banks to launch what became the UNEP Financial Inquiry. While work in green finance has been underway for years, it has gained momentum and tremendous policy importance since 2015, with both the Paris Climate Agreement and the Sustainable Development Goals (SDGs) moving discussions from the billions needed to remediate pollution and other problems, to the trillions in the financial system that need to embed core environmental and sustainability standards. The so-called shift from "billions to trillions" has shifted earlier green finance discussions from smaller-scale project finance issues, to far more ambitious systemic changes needed to realize a financial system fit for the purpose of building sustainability.

II. Green Finance in China

China has been advancing green finance for a decade. The evolution of different building blocks, such as regulatory reform, to innovation, such as green bonds is summed in a 2017 report – *Establishing China's Green Financial System*, by Simon Zadek and Wang Yao. A key feature of China's leadership is the emphasis on policy coherence, in which a *systemic* approach to green finance includes a range of institutions – for example the People's Bank of China, the China Banking Regulatory Commission, the China Securities Regulatory Commission, the China Insurance Regulatory Commission and others – to coordinate rules, market signals, risk instruments and innovative products offerings. Underscoring this approach, the Third Plenum of the 18th CPC Congress stressed that "efforts must be made to establish a systematic and full-fledged institutional system of ecological civilization for the protection of eco-environment."

An important launching of China's green finance work occurred in 2014, at the Eco-Forum Global meeting. The Eco-Forum Global is China's state-level international discussion forum in which a broad range of environmental protection, conservation, big data and other issues are jointly explored by both Chinese and international expert.

Domestic Convener Green Finance Task Group. There could not have been a more able lead than Ma Jun, who, in September 2017, was named as UNEP's Special Advisor on Green Finance.

The mandate of the Task Force was broad, impressive and ambitious from the outset. The deputy governor of the People's Bank of China called on it not only to identify green finance pathways that avoided pollution and other forms of ecological harm, but also to identify financial products and practices that support positive green investments. This focus on both environmental risks and opportunities has been a crucial focus of the ongoing work of the UNEP Financial Inquiry. By bringing in a range of key financial institutions and agencies, including the China Banking Regulatory Commission, the Ministry of Finance and China's Industrial Bank, the

agenda of the Task Force was intentionally multi-layered and crosscutting. The scope of its work was equally broad, to include green banks, green bonds, green insurance, green IPOs, green credit rating, environmental liabilities for banks, green information disclosure, a green database, a green investor network, green outward-bound investments from China, green asset securitization, testing of banks' resilience for environmental risks, and encouraging Chinese banks to adopt and implement the Equator Principles.

III. Using Existing Products, New Products and Blending Finance

In 2015, the Task Force released its report, *Establishing China's Green Financial System*. An important focus of the report was on practical results, and then a series of specific action items and recommendations were detailed for each of its working themes. Dr. Jun also identified six overarching characteristics that were needed to advance China's green financial system:

1. China's green financial system should not only contain measures to restrict polluting investments, but also comprise mechanisms to encourage green investments;

2. The system should not only rely on existing banking channels to promote green credits, but also consider creating new green lending and investment institutions;

3. The system should reduce reliance on government administrative orders, and instead favour market-based signals to steer private capital towards green industries;

4. The system should both provide green loans as well as promote new green financing channels and products, notably green bonds,

green stocks, green funds, green insurance and carbon emission trading;

5. The system should leverage public financial and legal mechanisms to attract and accelerate private capital. This emphasis on blended finance, which was underscored at the 2015 Finance for Development summit in Addis, is important both to avoid increased pressure on public budgets as well as pulling more capital into green industries. Dr. Jun noted that some government signals can shift the investment behaviour of private financial flows.

6. The system should provide support enabling financial infrastructure to allow green finance to expand, including databases, green credit ratings and environmental information disclosure rules to help investors evaluate the environmental impacts of their investments. Only after environmental information and costs become readily available to potential investors can the green finance system achieve success in guiding investments into green industries through market mechanisms.

These six key principles together provide a very valuable roadmap in how to deploy both existing agencies and regulations, as well as drive innovation to scale-up new products, such as green bonds.

IV. China's Leadership in G20 Green Finance Work

Following the 2015 report of the Task Force, China's Presidency of the G20 led to the creation of the G20 Green Finance Study Group, with Dr. Jun serving as the co-convener together with the Bank of England and the UNEP Financial Inquiry. The mandate of the G20 Study Group was to "identify institutional and market barriers to green finance, and...develop options on how to enhance the ability of the financial system to mobilize private capital for green investment."

In 2016, the G20 Green Finance Study Group forwarded a number of objectives in order to help meet its mandate. The G20 Study Group recommendations focused both on scaling up specific new products, like green bonds, increase the use of relevant voluntary principles related to green finance, strengthen environmental risk disclosure, and share common, systemic risks across the financial services sector. In order to help frame these efforts, the G20 Group recommended the need to identify signals and frameworks, notably the Sustainable Development Goals and the Paris Agreement, to inform investors of the trends away from dirty to cleaner, greener and low-carbon investments[1].

V. Progress and Steps Ahead

At the UN Climate Week meetings in New York in September 2017, the CEO of a global investment bank concluded at a World Economic Forum meeting that the financial sector was now at a "tipping point" in moving towards low-carbon and zero-carbon pathways. Underscoring this point, in November 2017, Norway's sovereign wealth fund, valued at approximately US$1 trillion, announced it was dumping all of its oil and gas holdings to decrease the financial risk due to the "permanent drop in oil and gas princes." This followed a 2016 decision by the Fund to exclude over 50 coal-related companies from their portfolio. While the coal decision was based on the Fund's internal ethical and corporate social responsibility guidelines, the oil and gas decision was crucially based entirely on economic analysis that pointed to shrinking returns on investment in the oil and gas sector.

VI. Shifting Markets and Enhanced Disclosure

A big question is to what extent the Norwegian Fund decision will have ripple effects across other investors and markets? According to analysis by the International Renewable Energy Agency (IRENA), financing of renewable energy has increased significantly in the past decade, despite year-to-year volatility, but remains largely underfinanced in relation to conventional energy sources. Many reasons explain the financing gap between conventional and clean energy solutions, including the persistence of fossil fuel subsidies to support consumption and production of fossil fuels. Estimates by IISD's Global Subsidies Initiative (GSI) place annual subsidies at more than $400 billion a year, four times the total amount of subsidy price support provided to renewable energy.

One way to think about the Norwegian example is within the broader systemic framework outlined in the 2015 China report and 2016 G20 recommendations. One announcement in itself will not shift markets. But viewing that together with other initiatives

---

[1] "Provide strategic policy signals and frameworks: Country authorities could provide clearer environmental and economic policy signals for investors regarding the strategic framework for green investment e.g., to pursue the Sustainable Development Goals (SDGs) and the Paris Agreement." Ibid.

underscores the growing momentum towards green finance. One notable step forward is the July 2017 report of the Task Force on Climate-Related Financial Disclosures of the Financial Stability Board （FSB）. The recommendations address all major actors in financial services, calls for the disclosure of both actual and potential climate-related risks, calls for clear metrics to measure and compare risks, and internal strategies to mitigate those risks.

The FSB immediately welcomed the recommendations of the Task Force, and mandated it to continue its work. Immediately, several large private investor groups such as Blackrock and Vanguard, have given notice of their move towards enhanced climate risk disclosure. Over the medium term, the Task Force will likely redefine materiality related to climate risk, and in turn provide an opportunity for the approximately 380 mandatory and voluntary corporate reporting platforms to converge around climate risk.

VII. Innovative Green Products

While momentum is underway to identify, disclose and manage climate risk, comparable progress is needed – as Dr. Jun noted in 2015 – in building positive momentum towards green investments. An impressive area of progress is the rapid growth in green bonds: today, China is the largest issuer of green bonds in the world, followed by France and the United States. In November 2017, Moody's reported that green bonds reached US$95 billion, an increase of almost 50 percent from the previous year. In order to ensure the continued growth and

legitimacy of green bonds, work is needed to identify both the environmental benefits and impacts of green bonds versus vanilla bonds, and help identify comparable metrics across different bonds issuers.

IISD's work on green finance in China to date has comprised research on green bond design and issuance-related issues, green securitisation and tax treatment to help scale-up green investment, extending China's leadership on green finance, noting that green bonds will have an increasingly important role in blending public-private finance to accelerate a transition to a green economy, based on the assumption that as much as 85 percent of the total financing needed to green the economy will come from private sources.

One challenge related to green bonds leveraging is aligning bond issuance to the size of the project. The IISD report notes that the typical size that an institutional investor is looking for is a bond issuance is greater than $200 million, with markets preferring larger scale issuances around US$1 billion. In China, bond issuance size is typically in the range of $100 million, and for many green projects – green infrastructure, integrated water resource management, reforestation and climate-related sequestration credits – project size may be much smaller than the $100 million threshold. One way to align potential financing to project needs entails bundling small-scale projects, using for example asset-backed securities. However, bundling in turn presents additional challenges related to measuring the environmental benefits of green versus vanilla bonds. Other challenges and solutions examined in the IISD paper are noted below:

Challenge	Appropriate Solution
Small—scale projects and lack of aggregation instruments create barriers to achieving issuance scale	Green securitisation, including the use of standardised loan contracts and financial warehouses
Low credit—ratings for potential green bond issuers create barriers to attracting institutional investors	Credit enhancement and green securitisation
Low credit—ratings for green projects create barriers to attracting institutional investors	Credit enhancement
Green bond investment must be increased to keep pace with scaling up of green bond issuance	Tax incentives for green bonds, including green asset—backed securities

While the scale of green bonds continues to expand, there are many other examples of innovation in financial products that embed green characteristics. One recent example is the issuance by the U.S.-based Citi Group of an Efficiency Services Agreement (ESA), similar in design to a more familiar power purchase agreement used extensively to finance renewable energy projects. The ESA supports the financing of energy efficiency– in essence financing avoided energy use through efficiency upgrades like LED lighting. The pilot energy efficiency project announced in the fall 2017 is expected to be scaled up to a US-wide product offering by Citi and partners.

VIII. Signals and Frameworks

Almost weekly, there are other examples of innovative financial products being launched and scaled to support the Paris Agreement. While this innovation continues, the G20 recommendation that the financial sector take into account broader signals and important frameworks, such as the Sustainable Development Goals (SDGs), is noteworthy. While it is still early days for the SDGs, they continued to gain momentum at the country-level, with some leading private sector actors, as well as with the international system more broadly.

A key underlying characteristic of the SDGs is their emphasis on holistic, integrated policy action that moves beyond singular, specialized action. A further key characteristic is its emphasis on transformative change to respond to urgent global ecological degradation, systemic economic uncertainty (for example the future of the multilateral trading system) and various social concerns, for example income inequality within and between countries. As such, the SDGs have been called the new Bretton Woods systems for the twenty-first century.

One emerging economic framework that China has helped accelerate involves the reform of standard economic measures like Gross Domestic Product (GDP). While GDP is perhaps the most well-known indicator ever devised, its objective was never to measure progress beyond specific estimation of asset values and income flows. GDP is not by definition holistic, is not intended to measure the values of key ecological endowments or pollution damage costs (other than remediation-related expenditures and income), nor indicators such as human

development or collective well-being. Nor is GDP intended to signal future risks.

There are various examples of beyond GDP work, including a global estimate by UNEP Inclusive Wealth methodology, guided by the economic models, data and methods of Cambridge economist Sir Partha Dasgupta and others. The first in-country analysis based on UNEP's global work was led by IISD, with the 2016 release of the report *Comprehensive Wealth in Canada*[1], which measured national progress in one country（Canada）, looking beyond income flows to measure four pillars of genuine wealth – human capital, natural capital, human capital and social capital. The findings brought forward a quite different picture of sustained progress, compared what GDP was equipped to provide. For example, by showing a decline of almost 25 percent in natural capital over three decades, the *Comprehensive Wealth* report – which is based on data, statistics and clear methods as opposed to scenarios and models – provides a clear policy signal that Canada （and likely other natural resource-based countries） could not repeat into the future their past economic development trajectories.

This type of frameworks can help create a larger economic context for green investments. That China has championed the notion of progress beyond GDP reflects another example of its commitment to an integrated, forward-looking and innovative area of policy innovation.

IX. Concluding Remarks

The pace of innovation in China in supporting green finance is indeed impressive. Many countries and institutions are now looking to Chinese leadership on this critical issue. China continues to pilot both new policies as well as pilot zones to test them. On June 2017, for example, China's State Council announced green finance pilot zones in Zhejiang, Jiangxi, Guangdong, Guizhou and Xinjiang. The lessons that emerge from these pilot zones, particularly in realizing a coherent system to accelerate green are of critical importance both for China and the world.

References：

[1] Financial Stability Board. 2017."Final Report: Recommendations of the Task Force on Climate-Related Financial Disclosures."https://www.fsb-tcfd.org/wp-content/uploads/2017/06/FINAL-TCFD-Report062817.pdf.

[2] G20 Green Finance Study Group. 2016. "G20 Green Finance Synthesis Report."http://unepinquiry.org/wp-content/uploads/2016/09/Synthesis_Report_Full_EN.pdf.

[3] IISD. 2017. *Comprehensive Wealth*. http://www.iisd.org/comprehensivewealth/en/.

[4] International Institute for Green Finance and UNEP. 2017."Establishing China's Green Financial System: Progress Report 2017."http://unepinquiry.org/wpcontent/uploads/2017/11/China_Green_Finance_Progress_Report_2017_Summary.pdf.

[5] International Monetary Fund. 2015. *From Billions to Trillions: Transforming Development Finance Post-2015 Planning for Development: Multilateral Development Finance*. IMF. http://

---

[1] IISD,（2017）, Comprehensive Wealth, http://www.iisd.org/comprehensivewealth/en/.

siteresources.worldbank.org/DEVCOMMINT/ Documentation/23659446/DC2015-0002（E） FinancingforDevelopment.pdf.

[6] IRENA. n.d. *Finance and Investment.* http:// www.irena.org/financeinvestment.

[7] Jinping, Xi. 2017. "Secure a Decisive Victory in Building a Moderately Prosperous Society in All Respects and Strive for the Great Success of Socialism with Chinese Characteristics for a New Era."19th National Congress of the Communist Party of China, http://www.xinhuanet.com/english/download/ Xi_Jinping's_report_at_19th_CPC_National_ Congress.pdf.

[8] Metrus Energy. 2017. *Metrus Closes Massive Efficiency-as-a Service Project for New Fortune 100 Technology Customer.* http://blog.metrusenergy.com/metrus-closes- massive-efficiency-as-a-service-project-for- new-fortune-100-technology-customer/.

[9] People's Bank of China and UNEP. 2015. "Establishing China's Green Financial System: Final Report of the Green Finance Task Force of China." http://unepinquiry.org/wpcontent/ uploads/2015/12/Establishing_Chinas_Green_ Financial_System_Final_Report.pdf.

[10] Weihui, Dai, Sean Kidney, and Beate Sonerud, 2016, *Roadmap for China: Using Green Securitisation, Tax Incentives and Credit Enhancements to Scale Green Bonds.* IISD and Climate Bonds Initiative.

中国绿色金融体系的发展回顾与展望

■ 王　遥　罗谭晓思[1]

摘要：自《关于构建绿色金融体系的指导意见》（以下简称《指导意见》）出台以来，除了中央和地方层面政策的持续推动，中国在绿色金融的产品、机构、标准、方法等方面取得了许多重要的进展，并在推动绿色金融国际合作中扮演着越来越重要的角色。未来，中国的绿色金融进程不仅将决定本国的绿色发展程度，而且将对全球绿色经济转型构成相当的影响。本报告基于《指导意见》的体系建设目标，从政策、产品、市场基础设施等多个维度，对这一年多来中国绿色金融发展进行综述和评议，并就未来发展提供一些建议与展望。

根据预测，为实现绿色经济和生态文明制度体系建设的发展目标，到2020年，中国每年至少需要3万亿—4万亿元以上的绿色投资，且其中至少85%需来源于社会资本投入[2]。作为撬动社会资本、助推绿色经济转型升级的金融解决方案，绿色金融在中国逐渐兴起。2016年8月31日，中国人民银行、财政部等七部委联合发布了《指导意见》，第一次系统性地推出了绿色金融的官方定义、激励机制、披露要求、绿色金融产品发展规划和风险监控措施，标志着服务于绿色发展目标的金融供给侧结构性改革正式启动。自此，中国的绿色金融一改之前的碎片化发展状态，开始以体系的形式纳入政策和监管框架，绿色融资和

绿色金融产品创新也在政策激励下取得了快速发展。

一、中国绿色金融体系发展概况

自2007年以来，中国绿色金融先后历经了初始、深化和全面推进三个阶段，在政策、产品、市场基础设施等方面均实现了一定程度的发展。

顶层设计全面综合，地方试验打造差异化示范样本。目前，中国已明确提出了绿色金融体系的战略框架与政策信号，其中既包括顶层设计的综合方案——《指导意见》，也涵括各部门根据分工方案所推出的绿色金融专项政策及实施

---

[1] 王遥系中央财经大学绿色金融国际研究院院长、中国金融学会绿色金融专业委员会副秘书长；罗谭晓思系中央财经大学绿色金融国际研究院研究员。

[2] 马骏，绿色金融：中国与G20，2016年9月。

细则。2017年6月14日，国务院决定在浙江、江西、广东、贵州、新疆5省（自治区）设立绿色金融改革创新试验区，并随后发布了各试验区的总体实施方案。此举旨在通过确立五个各具差异化特征的试验区，探索不同背景的地方绿色金融体系建设模式，从而为全国层面推进绿色金融积累多样化的实践样本。当前不仅五个试验区落地实践取得初步进展，而且有超出10个非试验省区相继发布绿色金融政策框架，积极承接国家绿色金融顶层规划。

绿色信贷根基扎实，稳步推进。作为中国起步最早的绿色金融领域，绿色信贷在中国绿色金融体系构建中也发挥着基础性作用。中国现已建立了由绿色信贷指引、绿色信贷统计制度与绿色信贷考核评价体系三部分组成的制度框架，并正在探索将绿色信贷业绩评价纳入宏观审慎评估（MPA）体系之中。绿色信贷规模保持稳定，截至2016年底，中国21家主要银行金融机构的绿色信贷余额达到7.51万亿元，同比增长7.13%，占各项贷款余额的8.83%。此外，银行业金融机构在制定绿色信贷配套政策的基础上，开发绿色信贷产品达50余类，服务范围包括绿色资产抵质押融资与节能减排、新能源等绿色项目融资。

绿色债券亮点突出，市场基础设施日益完善。随着绿色债券政策体系不断完善与中国经济绿色转型的需求日益明确，中国一跃成为全球最大的绿色债券市场之一。2017年，中国在境内外发行的绿色债券达到2512.14亿元，占全球同期绿色债券发行量的32.16%[1]。在所有绿色债券种类中，金融债发行规模独大。中国绿色债券第三方专业评估和评级市场发展迅速，市场公信力逐渐增强，并有多家市场机构相继开发绿色债券指数工具。

绿色股票指数初具规模。截至2017年6月30日，绿色股票被动型指数基金达到22只，总规模为73.91亿元[2]；绿色开放指数型基金则达到25只，共计252.84亿元[3]。同时，强制性环境信息披露制度在环保部、证监会等部门的合作下稳步推进。随着环保企业上市的政策支持力度不断提升，绿色企业上市融资与再融资积极性不断提高，尤其在污染防治领域。

绿色基金与PPP发展迅速。当前各类绿色基金蓬勃发展，截至2016年底，中国基金业协会备案的绿色基金共265只，其中绿色产业基金达215只，2016年的新增基金数为121只[4]。在这些基金中，无论政府是否参与，"市场化运作"已普遍成为基本管理原则。PPP模式在绿色产业中的运用也不断深化。在财政部、国家发展改革委关于支持PPP的系列政策性文件推动下，PPP模式在绿色基础设施、污染治理和资源高效利用等公共服务领域的应用持续深入，资源组合开发、环境合同绩效管理、资源化利用等绿色PPP收费机制开始受到中央与地方政府的政策支持。

绿色保险产品创新活跃。一是环境污染强制责任保险制度建设稳步推进，由环保部与保监会联合发布的《环境污染强制责任保险管理办法》进入征求意见阶段，2016年各地试点的环境污染责任保险保费收入达到2.8亿元左右，提供风险保障超出260亿元。二是绿色保险产品对于经济的助推作用不断展现，其中既包括环境风险保障范

[1] 数据来源：中央财经大学绿色金融国际研究院（2018），中国绿色债券市场2017年度总结。
[2] 中央财经大学绿色金融国际研究院根据Wind公开数据进行整理。
[3] 中央财经大学绿色金融国际研究院根据Wind公开数据进行整理。
[4] 数据来源：中国人民大学重阳金融研究院（2017），中国绿色金融发展报告。

围的创新延伸（如生猪保险与病死猪无害化处理联动机制、气象指数保险、科技保险、太阳能发电指数保险等），也包括建立与其他绿色资质的联动机制以实现对绿色产品的增信功能（如绿色建筑保险、"政银保"合作农业贷款模式、专利质押融资保证保险等）。三是通过技术与模式的创新，绿色保险的环境风险管理能力不断提升，例如引入第三方专业服务机构定期开展"环保体检"、运用无人机、卫星遥感等实时风险监测与防控技术进行环境风险减量管理。

环境权益交易体系持续探索绿色定价机制。从"十二五"规划开始，中国相继推出了碳排放权、排污权、节能量/用能权和水权等四种主要的环境权益。目前，各环境权益交易市场的所处阶段有较大差异：碳排放权交易已日益成熟，全国碳市场于2017年12月19日正式启动，将首先纳入发电行业，并在一年配额模拟交易期后，正式开展配额现货交易；排污权有偿使用和交易制度已在11个省（自治区、直辖市）开展试点，2016年排污许可制改革开始，进一步落实了企业的总量控制责任；节能量/用能权、水权交易均已启动省份的探索试点，但整体仍处于制度建设初期。

环境风险分析成为研究重点。通过开展系列环境风险分析和管理框架研究，环境压力测试开始纳入企业与金融机构的投资实践中，例如工商银行先后对火电、水泥与钢铁行业进行了信用风险影响的环境压力测试。中财绿金院将沪深300作为一个资产组合，分别进行了碳风险、水风险、大气污染风险和环境处罚风险带来资产组合损失的环境压力测试。作为环境风险分析体系的重要制度支撑，强制性环境信息披露制度建设在《指导意见》发布后正式提上日程。随着发布社会责任报告的上市公司逐渐增多，以及IPE等公共环境信息披露平台的兴起，公共环境数据来源也日益丰富。

国际合作全面推进。在2016年G20峰会上，中国作为轮值主席国，历史性地将绿色金融列为G20议题，并提议设立了中英担任共同主席的G20绿色金融研究小组。自此，中国不仅主动设置国际绿色金融议题，而且深度参与可持续发展目标（SDGs）、《巴黎协定》等重大国际议题，努力推动全球绿色金融的交流合作。此外，中国广泛开展了与英国、卢森堡、美国、德国等国家在绿色金融研究、能力建设、标准国际化等方面的合作，并通过积极发行境外绿色债券、联合推出绿色指数型产品等方式促进跨境资本流动。同时，中国政府与业界已开始重视对外投资全产业链的绿色化，中国的绿色投资实践逐步走向国际。

二、中国绿色金融体系面临的挑战

绿色金融是一项涉及多部门、依托多领域配套政策的系统工程。虽然中国绿色金融政策框架已初步建成、市场也初具规模，但距离金融体系绿色化的目标仍任重道远。当前中国绿色金融体系主要面临以下挑战：

一是相关法律依据有待建立健全。在一些绿色金融领域，由于相关立法的缺失，权责不明晰，致使无法从法律制度层面构成强制力约束，因而使得绿色投融资的风险收益难以预期。以PPP模式为例，由于缺乏高位阶的立法规范，导致PPP模式本身与中国国内的现行法律法规之间存在大量冲突，各种显性或隐性的合规风险层出不穷。这对于企业社会资本方而言则意味着巨大的投资风险。为了规避此等风险，社会资本往往不得不通过"固定回报""明股实债"等"违规"方式锁定投资收益，给PPP项目的合规性、双方合作的稳定性都带来不利影响。

二是绿色金融相关标准亟待统一。目前，中国在绿色金融监管层面及地方实践层面均存在"绿色"定义不一致的问题，致使"洗绿""漂绿"风险较高。信息统计层面，环境信息披露制度、绿色金融统计与评估制度尚且缺乏统一的口径，致使绿色投资以及政策评估缺乏有效的数据支撑。

三是绿色金融的能力建设有待增强。绿色金融体系的构建不仅有赖于各级政府绿色发展意识的提高及对绿色金融的深刻认识，也有赖于政府、资金需求和供给方、中介机构对环境风险的有效识别，以及分析与管理能力的提升。当前，地方政府普遍缺乏对当地绿色金融现状的认知，且缺乏必要的金融机构与专业人才集聚以推动绿色金融落地发展。大多数金融机构不仅尚未深刻认识到环境风险对于其投资回报率的影响，而且缺乏相应的技术与经验对环境风险进行识别、评估与管理。

四是政策环境有待进一步完善。绿色金融发展需要财税政策、货币政策、信贷政策和产业政策间的相互协调与配合，进而全方位强化绿色投融资的激励与约束机制。目前，各政策工具间仍缺乏有效的协调机制，实质性激励与约束措施仍待进一步出台。

五是国际合作仍存在一定障碍。虽然目前中国的绿色金融国际合作已取得显著成效，但仍存在一定的障碍亟待突破：首先，由于对中国的资金流动管制政策不熟悉，国际投资者普遍担忧其资金难以顺利流出中国市场；其次，由于各国在发展阶段、产业结构及资源环境承载力等方面的差异，各国绿色定义不同且缺乏可比性；再次，国际投资者所能获得的中国绿色资产信息有限，对中国绿色金融市场的了解不足。

三、中国绿色金融体系的未来展望

为充分发挥绿色金融对经济绿色转型的积极作用，未来还需着力完善体系建设，以建立绿色金融的长效发展机制：

一是建立健全绿色金融法律制度。一方面，需要在《商业银行法》《证券法》和《保险法》中加入"绿色"元素，如研究明确贷款人环境法律责任，诉讼资格和连带责任制度等；另一方面，对于环境权益交易、绿色PPP、绿色基金等领域确保立法先行，明确各绿色金融要素的法律属性以及利益相关方的权利与义务。

二是推进绿色金融标准化工程。关于绿色界定标准，国家发展改革委正在牵头制定国家《绿色产业目录》，这将成为全国统一"绿色"定义的基础。基于统一的"绿色"标准，中国需进一步构建绿色金融活动影响及测度的统计体系，并建立标准化的绿色金融评估机制，以引导绿色投资、帮助政策制定者和监管者进行政策效果评估。此外，通过推动绿色金融产品标准化，将有利于推进绿色资产证券化，进而盘活存量绿色资产，扩大绿色投融资规模。

三是加强利益相关方的能力建设。环境风险分析方面，监管机构、行业自律组织和绿金委可引导系统重要性金融机构率先开展环境风险分析与管理实践，并通过方法学开发与推广、公共环境数据改善等方式逐步增强全行业的环境风险管理能力；组织建设方面，在推动传统金融机构绿色化转型的同时，也推动建立专门的绿色金融机构与分部，并培育第三方绿色评级机构以增强投资者的环境风险识别能力；绿色投资者培育方面，通过构建绿色投资者网络、加强媒体宣传与舆论引导，提升市场的绿色投资意识；人才培养方面，绿金委、学术机构以及其他相关机构应着力推动专业人才的培育。

四是强化绿色金融的政策支持。一方面，将财政资金和政府信用更多运用到市场化绿色金融供给的激励上，充分发挥财政信用和财税政策撬动社会资本的能力。另一方面，通过加强环保执法、建立绿色金融产品与绿色资质间的联动机制，强化环境成本的内部化机制。同时，通过以

信息共享为基础，建立分工明确的跨部门协调机制，建立持续稳定的政策框架，确保绿色金融政策的统一性与连续性。

五是进一步深化绿色金融国际合作。外汇方面，通过释放明确的管制政策信息，并对外汇资金如何流入与流出提供透明而详细的指导，从而鼓励更多国际投资者通过有效途径投资中国市场；绿色定义方面，在保留各国特殊性的基础上，推动绿色定义基本框架的一致化，进而提高各国绿色定义的透明度和可比性；信息渠道方面，通过加强绿色金融数据库建设、开发国际化的绿色指数、投资者路演等方式，增加国际投资者掌握中国绿色金融市场信息的渠道，吸引国际投资者对中国绿色债券和绿色股票的投资。

随着绿色金融理念的推广，越来越多的国家开始将绿色金融纳入政策体系中。作为发展中国家代表，中国在绿色金融领域所达成的政策承诺、实践引领以及国际动员，已处于全球领先地位。未来，中国在不断推进绿色金融体系建设的同时，也将为其他国家，尤其是发展中国家，提供发展模式的经验借鉴。中国的绿色金融进程不仅将决定本国的绿色发展程度，而且将对全球绿色经济转型构成相当的影响。

The Progress and Outlook of China's Green Financial System

■ Wang Yao   Luo Tanxiaosi[1]

Abstract: Since the release of the *Guidelines*, aside from continuous policy implementation at central and local levels, China has made major progress in areas including green financial products, institutions, standards and methods, and has been playing an increasingly important role in facilitating international cooperation in green finance. In the future, China's green finance development process will not only determine the level of green development in China, but also exert considerable influence on the green transition of the world economy at large. This report takes stock of and reviews China's development of green finance over the past year in various dimensions including policies, products, and market infrastructure and offers recommendations and an outlook on future development.

According to estimates, in order to achieve the objectives of green development and ecological civilisation, China needs a minimum of RMB3-4 trillion each year in green investments before 2020, at least 85% of which needs to come from private capital.[2] As a financial solution to mobilise private capital and bridge the funding gap, green finance has gradually come to a rise in China.

On 31 August 2016, seven ministerial agencies including the People's Bank of China （PBC） and the Ministry of Finance jointly released the *Guidelines for Establishing the Green Financial System* （the "Guidelines"）, setting out, for the first time, the official definition of green finance, incentives, disclosure requirements, development plan for green financial products, as well as risk mitigation. This document marked the official initiation of supply-side financial structural reforms aiming to promote green development. The *Guidelines* also included green finance into China's policy and regulatory framework, putting an end to its previously fragmented

[1] Wang Yao，Director Genneral of International Institute of Green Finance,Cufe and Deputy Director General of Green Finance Comittee,China Society for Finance and Banking.Luo Tanxiaosi,Researcher of International Institute of Green Finance,Cufe.

[2] Ma Jun. （2016）. Green Finance: China and G20.

development. Spurred by policy incentives, green financing and green financial product innovation have seen a rapid development ever since.

I. The Latest Progress of China's Green Financial System

China's green finance has been through three stages successively—initial, consolidation and implementation stage since it was started at 2007, making impressive progress in policy framework, product innovation and market infrastructure.

(i) Comprehensive top-level design, with differentiated local pilot practices

Currently, China has established a strategic framework and policy guidelines for the green financial system, including both a comprehensive plan for the top-level design— the Guideline, and implementing rules released by the corresponding responsible ministries.

On 14 June 2017, the State Council decided to set up pilot zones for green finance reform and innovation in Zhejiang, Jiangxi, Guangdong, Guizhou and Xinjiang, followed by overall plans for each pilot zone jointly released by seven ministerial agencies. By establishing these five distinct pilot zones, China aims to explore different development models for the local green financial system against different backgrounds, thus offering diverse practical samples for promoting green finance across the country. Not only have the five pilot zones achieved initial progress, but over 10 other provinces and autonomous

regions not covered by the pilot programme have also released policy frameworks on green finance.

(ii) Green credit: solid foundation and sound development

As the field that pioneers green finance in China, green credit serves as the foundation of China's green financial system. At the national level, an institutional framework consisting of guidelines, statistical system and evaluation system has been created in China. More efforts are being made to include green credit performance evaluation into the Macro Prudential Assessment (MPA) system.

The size of green credit remains stable, with the outstanding green credit of 21 major banking and financial institutions in China amounting to RMB7.51 trillion by the end of 2016, a year-on-year increase of 7.13%, and accounted for 8.83% of all outstanding loans. Banking institutions have been active in formulating their own policy framework. Under such a framework, they have developed over 50 green credit products, covering services such as accepting green assets as collateral or pledges, and financing energy efficiency, emission reductions, and renewable energy projects.

(iii) Green securities: prominent in a strengthening market infrastructure

With improved policy systems for green bonds and an increasingly pressing need to pivot towards a green economy, China has become one of the world's largest green bond markets. In 2017, China issued a total of RMB251 billion worth of green bonds in both the domestic and overseas market, accounting for 32.2% of global green bond issuance[1]. Among the diversifying green bond market, financial bonds make up the largest proportion of issuance. Meanwhile, third party verification and rating market grows rapidly with increasing market credibility, and multiple green bond index instruments have been developed.

In terms of green stocks, green stock indexes start to take shape. By 30 June 2017, there were 22 green stock passive index funds with a total size of RMB7.391 billion[2]; and 25 green open-end index funds with a total size of RMB25.284 billion[3]. Also, environmental information disclosure has been facilitated jointly by the Ministry of Environmental Protection along with the China Securities Regulatory Commission. With increasing policy support for the listing of environmental enterprises, green enterprises are enthusiastic about Initial Public Offering（IPO）financing and follow-on offerings, particularly in the field of pollution control.

（iv）Green funds and public–private partnerships（PPP）: rapid development with effects to be seen

Various types of green funds have developed vigorously in China. By the end of 2016, a total of 265 green funds were registered with the Asset Management Association of China, of which 215 were green industry funds and 121 were established in 2016[4]. Regardless of whether governments take part in these green funds or not, they are generally operated under a market-oriented principle.

PPP model is also extensively applied in the green industry. The Ministry of Finance and the NDRC released a host of documents to support and guide the PPP model, resulting in its broader adoption in public service fields such as green infrastructure, pollution control and resource efficiency. The combined development of resources, the performance management of environmental contracts, the recycling of waste and other paid-use mechanisms have begun to receive policy support from central and local governments.

（v）Green insurance: an innovative market seeking greater coverage

Firstly, the mandatory pollution liability insurance system continues to make steady progress. The *Measures for the Administration of Mandatory Pollution Liability Insurance*, jointly released by the Ministry of Environmental Protection and China Insurance Regulatory Commission（CIRC）, are undergoing public consultation and will soon be promulgated. In 2016, the premium income of pilot environmental pollution liability insurance reached approximately RMB280 million with a risk coverage worth over RMB26 billion.

Secondly, product and service innovation has increasingly driven the green economy, including both innovative extension of the insurance coverage of environmental risk （such as index-based climate insurance, technology insurance and solar radiation index insurance）, and the established linkage between green insurance and other

[1] IIGF of CUFE （2018）. Annual Progress Report of China's Green Bond Market 2017.

[2] Provided by the IIGF of CUFE based on public data by Wind.

[3] Provided by the IIGF of CUFE based on public data by Wind.

[4] Chongyang Institute for Financial Studies （2017）. China Green Finance Progress Report, , Renmin University of China.

green-related qualifications so as to fulfil credit enhancement functions for green products （such as green building insurance, "government-bank-insurer" cooperative agricultural loans and guarantee insurance for patent pledge financing）.

Thirdly, with application of new technology and innovative mode, the environmental risk management capability of the insurance sector continues to improve. Typical practices include introducing third-party institutions to periodically carry out "environmental health examinations", and employing real-time risk monitoring and control technologies, such as drones and satellite remote sensing.

（vi）Environmental credit trading: exploring and improving the green pricing mechanism

Since the release of the 12th Five-Year Plan, China has successively introduced four major environmental credits, namely carbon emission allowances, pollution rights, energy savings/energy use certificates and water rights. At present, the discrepancies between the development stage of each environmental credit trading schemes are quite large.

The carbon trading market is relatively mature, with the national carbon market officially launched by 19th Dec 2017. Utilities will be the first industry covered in the market, and it will test out the trading system by mock-trading credits for a year before initiating spot trading. As for pollution rights, the paid use and trading system has been implemented in 11 pilot provinces, municipalities and autonomous regions. The pollution permit system was launched in 2016, allowing enterprises to further fulfil their responsibility of total emission control. Both the energy-involved trading and water trading have

already launched their piloting programme, but they are still at the initial stage of system establishment.

（vii）Environmental risks in the financial system: a key research subject to be promoted

Based on research carried out on environmental risk analysis and management framework, environmental stress testing is being incorporated into the investment practices of enterprises and financial institutions. The Industrial and Commercial Bank of China, for instance, carried out environmental stress testing for the impact of environmental elements on the credit risk of thermal power, cement, iron and steel industries. Using CSI 300 Index as an asset portfolio, the IIGF CUFE conducted environmental stress testing to measure the impact of carbon price risk, water resource risk and environmental penalty risk on the returns and market value of the index components.

As a significant safeguard for environmental risk analysis framework, mandatory environmental information disclosure has been officially put on the agenda after the release of the Guidelines. With an increasing number of listed companies releasing their social responsibility reports, and the growth of public environmental information disclosure platforms such as IPE, the sources of public environmental data have also diversified.

（viii）International cooperation: leading the global greening process

At the G20 Summit in 2016, as the rotating chair, China included green finance in the G20 agenda for the first time, and proposed to establish G20 Green Finance Study Group, which is now co-chaired by China and the UK. Since then, China has proactively initiated international topics on green finance, and has been deeply involved in the Sustainable Development Goals（SDGs）, the Paris Agreement and other major international initiatives, promoting global communication and cooperation on green finance.

Furthermore, China has worked with Germany, Luxembourg, the UK and the US in terms of research, capacity building and international standardisation concerning green finance, and has facilitated cross-border capital flow by actively issuing green bonds in overseas markets and jointly launching green index products. Meanwhile, the Chinese government and the business community have started to attach great importance to developing a green industry chain for outbound investment, globalising their green investment practices.

II. The Challenges Faced by China's Green Financial System

Green finance is a systematic programme involving multiple sectors and relying on supporting policies in different fields. Although the green finance policy framework has already established and the market starts to take shape, there is still a long way to go "green" the financial system. The main challenges include:

（i）The absence of relevant legislation

Due to the lack of legislation concerning some green financial services, there is no legally binding rights and responsibilities for stakeholders, leading to unexpected risk and return in green financing. For instance, without high-level legislation, the practices of PPP have conflicted with the current legal system

in multiple aspects, bringing about both explicit and inexplicit compliance risks. It may cause significant investment risks for social capital. As a result, social capital may require fixed return to minimise such uncertainties, causing unfavourable influences on the compliance and persistence of PPP projects.

（ii）The disharmony among different green financial standards

Currently, the lack of a clear definition for "green" makes it difficult to identify green projects during regulations and local practices, which would increase greenwashing risks. Furthermore, due to the inconsistent calibre of environmental information disclosure and green financial statistical and assessment system, data quality has yet to be improved to provide effective support for green investment and policy evaluation.

（iii）The underdeveloped capacity among stakeholders

The establishment of green financial system not only relies on raising the awareness and deepening the understanding of green development among governments at all levels, but also depends on gaining knowledge about green finance as well as improving capacities for governments, investees, investors, and intermediaries. Currently, most of the local governments are inadequately informed of their latest development in green finance, and are generally suffer a shortage of financial institutions and professionals which are necessary for implementation. As for environmental risk analysis, not only have the majority of financial industry been unaware of the impact of environmental risks on their return on investment（ROI）, but they also lack corresponding methodology and experience to identify, assess and manage

environmental risks.

(ⅳ) The policy environment yet to be improved

To enhance both incentive and restrictive mechanisms for green financial activities, it requires different policies to collaborate with each other, which may involve fiscal, taxation, monetary, credit and industry policies. Currently, there still lacks an effective coordination mechanism among different policy tools, with substantial incentives and restricts to be further introduced.

(ⅴ) Barriers existed in international cooperation

Despite China's remarkable achievements in international cooperation in green finance, the following concerns and obstacles remain: firstly, due to the lack of understanding of China's capital flow control policy, most international investors are concerned that their capital may not be able to flow out smoothly from the Chinese market; secondly, because of the discrepancies of development stage, industrial structure and environmental vulnerabilities among different countries, their definition of green varies from each other and are generally incomparable; thirdly, international investors have limited access to information of China's green assets, resulting in an insufficient understanding of China's green financial market.

Ⅲ. Outlook of China's Green Financial System

To maximise the effects of green finance on facilitating green economy transition, further efforts are needed to establish a long-term development mechanism for the green financial system.

(ⅰ) To establish and improve the legal basis for green finance

On the one hand, green elements should be incorporated into the Law on Commercial Banks, the Securities Law and the Insurance Law, such as clarifying lenders' responsibilities, litigation eligibility, and joint and several liabilities on environmental issues. On the other hand, legislation should be accelerated for environmental credit trading, green PPP, green funds, etc., so as to define their legislative attributes and the rights and obligations of stakeholders.

(ⅱ) To promote standardisation of green finance

Currently, the National Development and Reform Commission (NDRC) is leading the formulation of the Green Industry Catalogue, which will lay a foundation for a unified definition of "green". In this context, China could establish an nationwide statistical system to measure the flows and influences of green financial activities. Furthermore, a standardised assessment system for green finance could be further set up so as to guide green investment and provide policy evaluation for policymakers and regulators. Furthermore, standardised green financial products could boost green asset securitisation, therefore revitalising the stock of green assets and increasing the size of green financing.

(ⅲ) To facilitate capacity-building of stakeholders

Regarding environmental risk analysis, regulators, self-regulatory organizations and the GFC could guide systemically important financial institutions to first conduct environmental risk analysis and management. With development in the methodology and the quality of public environmental data platform, the practice should be further promoted across the industry. In terms of organisation development, it not only includes green transformation of traditional financial institutions, but also takes account of establishing specialised green finance institutions, branches and third-party green rating agencies. To promote green investment, it is favourable to build green investor network while also strengthening media coverage and public education on green finance. Meanwhile, the GFC, research institutes and other relevant institutions should put effort into professional education.

(iv) To enhance policy support for green finance

As for incentive measures, more fiscal funds and government integrity should be applied as stimulus for market supply of green finance, maximizing the role of fiscal credit and fiscal and taxation policy in leveraging private capital. As for restrictive mechanism, by improving law enforcement and developing linkage mechanisms between green financial products and other green-related qualifications, the internalisation of environmental cost could be further consolidated. In the meantime, it is highly necessary to promote interdepartmental coordination based on information sharing and clarified responsibilities, so as to ensure the consistency and sustainability of green finance policies with a stable policy framework.

(v) To further deepen international cooperation on green finance

Concerning foreign exchange, it is imperative to release clear policies and offer transparent and detailed guidance on the inbound and outbound flow of foreign capital, to encourage more international investors to invest in China via effective channels. Regarding the discrepancies of different countries' green definitions, the transparency and comparability of the distinctive definitions should be improved by harmonizing the fundamental framework of green definitions while also retaining the uniqueness of each country. In terms of information access, efforts should be made to improve the green finance database, develop international green indexes and conduct investor roadshows, thus expanding channels for international investors to access the information of China's green finance market and attracting them to invest.

With the awareness-raising of green finance concept, countries start to increasingly incorporate green finance into their policy system. As a typical developing country, China has today more than any other country taken policy commitments, advanced practice and mobilized international action on green finance. In the future, while China keeps carrying forward its establishment of green financial system, its experience and special development mode would also act as reference for other countries, especially for emerging markets. Not only will China's green finance development process determine its domestic level of sustainable development, but it will also exert considerable influence on the green transition of the world economy at large.